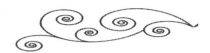

Praise for

What Every 6th Grader Needs to Know

10 Secrets to Connect Moms & Daughters

"At a time when so many barriers are straining mother/daughter relation-ships, and our daughter's esteem is being attacked from every side, "What Every 6th Grader Needs to Know" gives mothers the tools they need to communicate (even about the tough stuff). It gives daughters the confi-dence to know that *they* have what it takes to survive the unique transi-tional years. Whether your relationship with your daughter is strained, or you want to strengthen what is already strong, use this smart and savvy information. You and your girl(s) will learn how to *thrive* through the teen years."

--Heather Ann Johnson M.S. Adjunct Faculty, BYU, Mother of five girls

"With conflicting messages today, it's easy for moms and daughters to get confused and overwhelmed. This book bestows all the wisdom you want to pour into your daughter's heart and mind in a fun, non-threatening way. Dread turns into confidence as you realize you have the tools to face those teenage years TOGETHER and have a ball doing it."

--Rachel Skinner, Mother of nine, Social Worker

"This book provided a wonderful bonding experience for me and my daughter. As parents we always think we know how our child is doing. Then we get into a deep conversation and realize that compared to what we thought, they are doing either so much better or are suffering so much more. But they hold those feelings back to protect us. Sometimes they fear that talking about it means more pain, but this books shows that talking is healing, especially when we know how."

--Karrie Glazner, Mother of Three Wonderful Kids

What Every 6th Grader Needs to Know

10 Secrets to Connect
Moms & Daughters

by
Rachelle J. Christensen & Connie E. Sokol

What Every 6th Grader Needs to Know
10 Secrets to Connect Moms & Daughters

Original Cover Design: Kelli Ann Morgan
www.inspirecreativeservices.com
Cover Design © Peachwood Press

Interior book design by: Bob Houston eBook Formatting

Edited by: Stephanie Hengen

ISBN-13: 978-0692423301
ISBN-10: 0692423303

Published by Peachwood Press, April 2015

PEACHWOOD
Press

Table of Contents

My body is doing some weird things. Is that normal?

Some girls are developing faster than I am. Is there something wrong with me?

Am I supposed to be dating or in a relationship with a boy at my age?

If a boy doesn't like me, does that mean I'm not pretty? How can I get a boy to like me?

Why do boys try to act like they're all that and a bag of chips? Why are they annoying or aggressive?

How do I find true friends?

Should I try to make everyone else happy all the time?

How do I disagree with my friends? Will they hate me?

Should I believe the mean things others say about me?

Who makes "popular groups" popular?

Should I try to be, look, and act like everyone at school to fit in?

I'm starting middle school/junior high and I'm scared. How do I handle the change?

I'm afraid sixth-grade will be too hard. What if I fail?

Is it dumb to want to try out for things like honors classes, band, or sports? What if my friends aren't?

I think I know what I want to be when I grow up, but can I change my mind later?

I want to do great things, but I'm not very good at setting goals. What if I can't achieve them?

What if people think my dreams and goals are dumb?

Acknowledgements

Rachelle: I'm so grateful to my beautiful and amazing daughters, Gracie and Maggie. They are the inspiration for this book, and writing it has brought us closer together. Thank you girls for being willing to share your experiences and thoughts. My family is everything to me and I love being a mom. It's so hard and I make lots of mistakes, but I love my family more than anything! This book was such a fun process to create, and I want to thank my co-author, Connie, for believing in me and this concept. Her enthusiasm and ability to see my vision made this book happen. She is an incredibly talented lady, and I feel honored to have had the opportunity to write this book with her. I'd also like to thank my extended family for their continued support and encouragement of my writing. I'm grateful to my Heavenly Father for magnifying all of my small efforts and continually blessing me with goodness.

Connie: This book has been a wild adventure. From start to finish, it's taken mere weeks to complete—weeks filled with adrenaline, miracles, and inspired writing. Thank you to my fabulous family for love, support, and being willing guinea pigs. Most especially to my sweet Chloe, with whom I have triple-loved our connected chats and your insightful thoughts; what a memory-maker. And deep gratitude to Rachelle Christensen, a talented, cheerful, salt-of-the-earth woman, wife, and mother. With both of us focused on our families first, we shared the daily trial of finding writing time amidst kids' tantrums, emergencies, and every-day needs, and that made this journey a joy. And to my Heavenly Father who makes my beautiful life possible and thoroughly enjoyable.

Every book requires many people to make it a success. We thank our talented cover designer, Kelli Ann Morgan, for creating the fabulous cover and downloadable items for our website. Thanks to Bob Houston for his excellent typesetting and to our editor, Stephanie Hengen, who beautifully edited in record time.

Thank you to our early readers and contributors: Karrie and Haylee Glazner; Michelle and EllaAnne Packard; and Kami, Kiera, and Aubree Leonard.

Thank you to all of you wonderful moms and daughters who build relationships and connections that impact your family's lives for good. We understand how hard it can be for both mother and daughter during these transitional years. Every effort matters and makes a difference. We admire your dedication and are honored to be a part of you and your daughter's joyful journey.

Introduction: Just for Girls

Why should I read this book?

Life is busy, so we've worked hard to connect with sixth grade girls, listen to their questions, and find the answers to "10 Secrets" on growing up. We wrote this for both girls and moms to help you connect in happy, successful ways. And we've answered these questions as if speaking directly to your amazing girls.

Each section includes real life experiences, advice, tips for girls, notes for moms, and a bonus Kidspeak section written by a twelve-year-old girl. There are also practice scenarios and excellent tools to help you put what you learn to use. (Possible answers to these scenarios can be found at www.coachmom.org.) Check out the links for Super Sentence Cards and fill out the journal pages included at the end of each section.

From Rachelle: Just talking about this book with my daughters has helped us grow closer. As I worked on each section in this book, I kept finding opportunities to listen better and help reassure my daughters. The increased awareness of these real issues and concerns helped me to see things I might have missed before.

Take, for instance, the day my sixth-grader came home from school much quieter than usual. With four other kids running around the house, it could have been easily disguised. But I clued into her mood that something was bothering her, and I gave her space and freedom to tell me whatever she needed. About a half hour later, we were able to talk and enjoyed a connected, insightful conversation.

Each of these sections is filled with helpful discussion points and ideas. They may not perfectly fit every scenario you'll face, but we can guarantee that if you are studying and trying your best to work with your daughters, you'll find success. Together you will discover ways to connect and understand many new life changes in a more powerful and meaningful way than ever before.

Visit http://www.coachmom.org and www.conniesokol.com for great resources and additional information.

Hey Girls! Here's How to Use This Book:

Like every girl, questions run through your head that you want answered. But most of the time, you are too worried to ask or talk about your concerns. So, great job for reading this book. To find answers easier, we've asked other sixth-grade girls for their questions and written helpful answers. Now you don't have to worry, just read! We've included situations from girls just like you and guidance from experts who want you to know the secrets to growing up happy.

In each section you'll find cool tips, facts, ideas, and scenarios to help you through troublesome areas in your life. Be on the lookout for web addresses where you can go and download Super Sentence Cards and other great stuff (like at www.coachmom.org or www.conniesokol.com). Use the journal pages at the end of the chapter to jot down thoughts. But mostly, have fun discovering the secrets to growing up that you've always wanted to know!

Chapter 1: Beauty & Body Image

Scenario: *Yesterday Mia did her hair in a ponytail by herself and tied a purple ribbon around it. When she got to school, Tessa told her that she had tons of bubbles in her hair and the bow was crooked. Mia felt worried about her hair all day long. She was trying to look pretty and ended up feeling ugly.*

How do I know if I'm pretty?

The best way to handle tough situations is by tapping into your inner strength. We want to help you understand some important things about yourself: You are pretty, beautiful, cute, stunning, amazing, and wonderful because God created you and He doesn't make junk!

Have you ever noticed all of the colors in the world? There are thousands upon thousands of different shades and blends of each color. Think of the varieties around you right now: blue, purple, red, yellow, and more.

What makes those colors pretty? How do you *know* if a color is pretty?

You get to decide. Isn't that wonderful? You have the power to decide a favorite color. Already within you is the power to know that you are pretty. No one else gets to make that decision. You are in charge.

Right now, we invite you to embrace and accept your unique beauty. This kind of loveliness comes from the inside and then shows on the outside. We believe and know this about every girl out there—but do you believe it? Do you know it?

Try this simple but powerful action: Look in the mirror, smile, and say in a firm voice, "I am pretty." Say it with feeling. Say it a few times. Feel your voice get stronger and your heart feel happier. Believe it about yourself. Thinking good thoughts about yourself, as well as others, helps you become a brighter, happier person.

Recipe for Pretty:
1 cup Confidence
2 cups Smiles
1½ cups Kindness

To grow up pretty, add these ingredients to a healthy & nutritious lifestyle, pour it all into your unique mold, bake every day, & believe in yourself. Enjoy with a dash of laughter!

It's also true that we can't just believe that we are pretty without taking care of ourselves. You'll know you're pretty because you bathe or shower regularly and take good care of your body. So let's talk for a minute about that.

At age twelve, showering regularly means showering about three times a week. If you are into sports and dance, shower after practice to wash off the sweat and body odor. Whether or not you play sports, apply deodorant every day.

While in the shower, brush your hair and actively massage your scalp. This gets rid of dead skin that naturally occurs on anyone's head. After shampooing, rinse your hair thoroughly to remove leftover soap.

You don't have to wash your hair every day—in fact, you probably shouldn't. That's because your hair is protected by natural oils. Over washing your hair creates an imbalance in those oils, which can lead to problems with dry skin or dandruff as well as oily spots.

> ➤ Clean routines include showering at least three times a week and washing your hair about every third day.
> ➤ Use deodorant. There are either unscented or scented varieties. Go shopping with your mom and choose one you like and will wear every day.
> ➤ Change your underwear daily and remember to wash your bras every three or four days.
> ➤ Keep your clothes clean and washed regularly.

However, unless you sweat a lot or get dirty, you don't need to wash every shirt and pair of pants each time you wear them. Fold and put away clothes that can be re-worn. This is a form of recycling and is helpful to whoever does the laundry.

> ➤ Eat healthy and nutritious meals and snacks.

Include lots of yummy fruits and vegetables you like, such as grapes, apples, and tangerines. Limit the junk stuff like sugar, candy, and treats. Enjoy healthier versions if you can. For example, we love white cheddar popcorn, all natural cookies, and vegetable "french fries" that look like chips (so yummy!) Drink close to eight glasses of water a day—think "Water first!" Add lemon or cut strawberries for a fun zing. Following a healthy diet not only tastes good but creates pretty skin, a healthy body, and a happy you!

➢ Exercise regularly. Get out and move, just for fun. Go for walks, bike rides, shoot some hoops, jump rope, play sports. Find something that you enjoy and move every day, even if only for 10 minutes.

All of these steps to a beautiful body will help you to feel strong, healthy, and lovely. Feeling pretty works from the inside out, so enjoy taking care of yourself.

One last thought on beauty. Remember the many colors we talked about and how each is different but beautiful? That's YOU! Enjoy your special and beautiful look without comparing yourself to someone else.

We love what Rachelle's twelve-year-old girl shared: "I decided looking the same as everyone else isn't really *fitting in*." She learned to stand out in her own way. You can too!

Kidspeak: "I've decided that it doesn't take someone's approval or my friend deciding if I look pretty or not to make me feel pretty. It doesn't matter what other people do or say to me. I'm the one who's in charge of thinking, believing, changing, and being me! I can partly think I'm beautiful or *believe* I'm beautiful. I can force myself to be a different person and try to be someone else, or I can be happy for who I am."

Is a pimple or zit normal to have and will it go away?

Yes. Sad to say, pimples, zits, and other skin blemishes are totally normal for girls reaching the age of maturation and going through puberty. The good news? They go away.

- ✓ Here are a few tips to help your skin stay soft and clear:
- ✓ Don't pick at your blemishes.
- ✓ Wash your face every morning and night with a gentle cleanser.
- ✓ Eat a healthy diet and drink lots of water.
- ✓ Cut down on the amount of sugar you eat and don't drink soda.
- ✓ Wash your hands regularly. Try not to touch your face excessively as that will transmit germs, bacteria, and oils that can clog facial pores and increase breakouts.

If you have a painful red zit, use an ice cube wrapped in a wash cloth or tissue and hold it on the pimple to reduce swelling. Pat dry and use a tiny amount of cover-up to conceal the redness. Most zits go away in **three to five days**. If you pick at them, they often bleed and create scabs. And it increases the healing time to **seven to ten days**. So… no picking!

Some pimples will have yellow pus inside that often comes out on its own. If it's really large, massage the area gently with a warm cloth to release some of the pressure. Then ice the area, clean it, and apply concealer.

Even with your best efforts, some pimples are bound to surface. If you have already started getting your period, you may notice a few pimples each month around a certain time of your cycle. This is a side-effect of your body working to balance the different hormones needed for your menstrual cycle to occur. Don't give up hope! Follow the steps above and if you have lots of breakouts or overly large and painful zits, talk with your mom about seeing a dermatologist (skin doctor).

Kidspeak: "When I started getting a few pimples I was a little worried. Then it happened one day that I had (to me) a huge reddish pimple on my forehead. *Now* I was worried! I asked my mom if it would ever go away and how to prevent them. She told me almost all of the steps here on this page that you're reading. I use a special cleanser for my face and am careful not to pick at them. My mom helped me under-

Pimple Rescue Tip:
Cleanse the area.
Massage with a hot washcloth. Ice with an ice cube to reduce swelling. Apply witch hazel to speed healing.

Natural is Best: Studies show that wearing too much makeup can cause a breakout. Go for a more natural look and wash your face with a gentle cleanser.

stand that they are perfectly normal and I felt so relieved."

Do I need to wear makeup now?

The short answer is no, you don't have to. But if you really want to wear a *little* makeup ask your parents for their opinion and the family rule.

At school and around the neighborhood, you might notice some girls starting to wear makeup. Perhaps that creates a feeling of less-than—that your eyelashes aren't as full as you'd like or they're so blonde it's hard to see them. You might start feeling like it isn't okay to look natural.

Here's the part where we remind you to dig in your heels, stand up tall, and be proud of who you are.

If you don't want to wear makeup, then don't let others pressure you. Some girls begin as young as ten and eleven years old because of peers. Overall, that is a bit young and may not look age-appropriate on a young, active girl. Our (the authors') girls are all waiting until seventh grade to wear makeup.

Be happy and enjoy this time of your life. This is the last stage of childhood before you move into the teen years.

Want to wear mascara that isn't too bold? Try a shade of brown or dark blue instead of black.

Lip gloss can cheer up a look for minimal makeup. Swipe on a color that matches your skin tone—not something too red or too pink. One step brighter or darker than your natural lip color will accent your pretty smile.

If you do want to wear makeup and have checked with your parents, here are a few things to consider:

➢ Begin with a very basic makeup plan.

Wearing lip gloss is a simple and fun idea. Choose a shade that goes with your skin tone and the natural shade of your lips. If you like, it can be fun to wear a sheer gloss or neutral shade of lipstick for a special occasion.

➢ Add mascara, but not too much.

If it's too thick it makes your lashes appear clumpy or spidery. A basic black is usually the way to go, but even dark brown looks nice when your lashes are naturally light in color.

➢ Avoid using blush and foundation.

It leads to clogged pores. Remember, clogged pores lead to pimples and zits! Usually at age twelve, most girls have a natural blush anyway.

➢ Pay attention to how you feel when wearing makeup.

Decide if it's right for you. Maybe you don't want to be bothered with it after all at this age. Once you start wearing mascara, it is noticeable when you don't wear it, so keep that in mind.

➢ Give yourself permission to enjoy your natural beauty.

Sixth-grade is a fun, active time of your life. Don't be weighed down with other people's expectations. Do what feels right and natural to you as a person.

Kidspeak: "Many of my friends are starting to wear makeup and it made me feel a little uneasy. I really want to fit in but maybe right now makeup isn't really my thing. I want to wear makeup in 7th grade but a lot of my friends want me to wear it now. When I talked to my mom about it I finally felt good about my decision and decided looking the same as everyone else isn't really *fitting in.*"

> When girls feel bad about their looks, about 70% avoid normal daily activities (such as doing activities or attending school). Brighten someone's day by posting encouraging messages on your school's bathroom mirrors.
>
> Sign up for Mirror Messages. https://www.dosomething.org/facts/11-facts-about-teens-and-self-esteem

SUPER SENTENCES

I appreciate my _____(body part) because

_____!

I feel beautiful when _____.

I know I'm beautiful because _____.

Beauty, inside and out, to me means

_____.

One thing I can do to feel and become more beautiful, inside and out, is

_____

_____.

My Thoughts...

Chapter 2: Weight Worries

Scenario: *Several girls at your school are comparing their weight and checking with each other every day to see who weighs the least. You're feeling confused about the numbers they are sharing and wonder if you are at a normal weight.*

Should I be worried about my weight?

It's normal to think about your weight at this age. Because of the changes in your body, you're aware of growing taller, gaining more muscle, and developing in personal ways. However, it's never a good thing to worry about things we can't change. Worry only creates stress.

As young as age five, girls think curly hair needs to be straightened, and that it will make them happier and have more friends. Not so! Enjoy your curls which add variety and bounce. Studies show listening to your mother's positive comments on curls is actually one of the best ways to love them.

http://t.today.com/style/new-campaign-aims-help-girls-love-their-curls-1D80436325

Instead, it's best to empower yourself with knowledge and let go of fear. If you are worried about your weight, learn how to have proper health and nutrition. Add this to everyday movement or exercise and it becomes a life-long path to happy health. You can also talk with your doctor. Your doctor has tons of charts and graphs that give measurements for average weight and height for every age group and those charts don't lie. So if you, like most girls your age, fall within the average range then there's no need to worry about your weight!

Right about now you might be asking: *Aren't all girls supposed to weigh about the same? I don't weigh the same as other girls I know. Shouldn't I be even the least bit worried about that?*

Stop right there because that means you're not really listening.

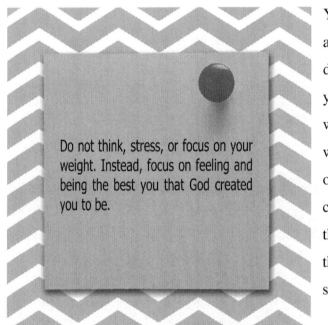

Do not think, stress, or focus on your weight. Instead, focus on feeling and being the best you that God created you to be.

You're thinking that all of that stuff doesn't apply to you, and you're still worried that you weigh more than the other girls in your class. Or that your thighs are bigger. Or that your arms are smaller.

Newsflash—this is important!—**everyone's body *is* different**. One girl is shorter, the other taller. One girl has larger muscles in her calves, another has smaller wrists. Just as some girls have naturally curly hair and others have straight hair, each facet of your body is different. When you compare yourself to someone else you will always come up short because you're not identical to anyone (unless you have a twin). *You are you* and there is only ONE you! The only person you should compare yourself to is yourself with the question: **Am I trying my best and loving myself?**

Okay, I know you still don't believe me, so with your parent's permission visit this website http://nccd.cdc.gov/dnpabmi/Calculator.aspx and check your Body Mass Index (BMI) for Children and Teens. You'll input your exact age to the month, your height, and your weight and get an instant report on your BMI. Most likely you will be in the normal healthy range. If you are in this

Link to Body Mass Index Calculator for Children & Teens

http://nccd.cdc.gov/dnpabmi/Calculator.aspx

Only 4% of women worldwide consider themselves beautiful. We need your help to change that! Try saying this affirmation every day: I'm thankful for my healthy beautiful body and happy to be me! (See "Super Sentences" downloads at the end of this chapter)

normal, healthy range you can stop worrying!

What if you aren't in the normal range? If you're underweight, consult your pediatrician as certain body types are petite and will be slightly underweight according to the BMI. However, these are actually normal for YOUR body type. The same is true if you are slightly overweight. Talk to your doctor for additional information.

The goal is to be within the healthy normal range for BMI for children. Stop worrying and start celebrating your good health!

Kidspeak: "I used to be worried about my weight when I was in grade school because I used to get teased by the other kids about it. There were days that I would come home in tears because the kids were so mean to me. The girls used to tell me I wasn't as pretty as them or wasn't as good as them, and I started to believe it myself. Even the boys would tease me and would pick on me. I have red hair and the boys would call me an ingabombi, which means orange-headed. I always wanted to change my hair color and begged my mom to let me dye my hair thinking that changing my appearance would change the way the others treated me. Now that I am in middle school, the kids are nicer to me. I am no longer bullied or teased. I don't let others decide what I think about myself and I know now that my looks don't determine who I am. I am who I am because of how I act. I choose who I want to be."

Should I go on diets with my friends?

It's a fact that some girls worry about their weight so much that they are willing to do extreme things about it. You might have noticed your friends talking about wanting to be skinnier. Maybe you've thought about skipping lunch or going on a diet with your friend. So let's talk for a moment about the word "influence," which means the effect of people, situations, or what you see, hear, or observe.

Every day you are surrounded by pictures on billboards, TV shows, and the internet of flawless models and "perfectly beautiful" people. But do you understand that these people are not real? If you saw them walking down the street you wouldn't recognize most of them. That's because their pictures were altered. The images you saw were edit-

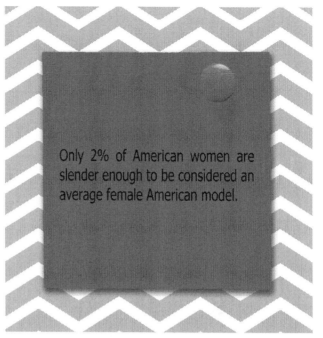

Only 2% of American women are slender enough to be considered an average female American model.

ed, air-brushed, and manipulated to the point that they don't look like the same person.

What that means is you and your friends might try to be skinnier to look like a certain model, pop star, or TV actress. But even *she* doesn't look like those images in real life.

A better use of your time, energy, and happiness is to focus on being your best self. Yes, eating healthy, exercising regularly, and feeling self-confident make the difference. Decide to love and respect your body by your actions and beliefs.

If you don't, you will constantly compare yourself to someone else. When you do that, you always come up wanting. Different doesn't always mean better or worse. No two people are alike and that is how it's supposed to be. People's opinions on the "right" body look will come and go. You get to choose your own opinion.

If you make healthy choices, live a good lifestyle, smile, and do good for others, beauty shines on your countenance. People will wonder what kind of makeup you wear to get that special "glow." You'll feel confident from knowing and feeling the true beauty that comes from joy and goodness, and it shows.

Make the choice today to stop obsessing about your weight, about whether your legs or thighs are skinny enough, or about whether your belly is flat enough. Don't go on diets or skip meals. Focus on being your best self and helping others. True happiness doesn't come from a flat belly. It comes from within.

> About 50% of high school girls with healthy weights diet because they feel "overweight". Don't fall into this trap of lifelong misery and body hatred. Take the Coach Mom challenge to accept your beautiful body and help others get the message of what real healthy bodies are.
> Visit Coachmom.org or www.back2basics.com for more!

Kidspeak: "I've always thought the pretty women on magazines and billboards were real people. I didn't really believe my mom when she told me they go in and change so many things about the person. Well, one day at school one of the teachers came in to give a lesson. I really liked this lesson and it helped me see things a lot differently. Afterwards the teacher showed the class a video about people on billboards and magazines. In the video they took a picture and changed the girl in it so much I thought my eyes would fall out. They made her neck longer, her eyes bigger, erased any pimples or bumps on her skin, changed her nose—everything! My mom was right! Now I listen to her and take her advice and I'm doing great. When you start loving your own body, you'll experience a change of your own."

"A lot of times I've wanted to go on a diet with my friends thinking it would make me skinnier. Well, I talked to my mom and really the only diet she said you should be going on is: cutting back on sugar, drinking more water and eating more fruits and vegetables! My mom said I was too young to be dieting and now I should just focus on cutting back on junk and eating healthier foods."

True words from Real Moms:
"I want to talk to you about this but it's important that you understand and believe me when I say I love you no matter what your size is. Now what is your biggest concern right now?"

"I understand that you are worried that your thighs are big, but they aren't. Your thighs are supporting the largest bone in your body—the femur. If they were any smaller, you would have a hard time running, jumping, skipping, and even walking."

How do I know if my mom is being nice or being honest about my weight?

Our moms love us so much and we know they want us to feel good about ourselves, right? Well, because of this, many moms get worried when their young daughters start asking about weight. This is an issue that sixth-grade girls shouldn't worry about, but sometimes they do.

True words from Real Moms:

"Your stomach is not supposed to be flat. Sure, we don't want fat rolls. But it's not realistic to have a completely flat stomach. When you sit down, especially after eating a meal, your stomach will stick out a little bit because that is what it is supposed to do."

After reading the section above, chat with your mom. Together you can visit the website with the BMI index for children and healthy weight. Tell your mom your true feelings and let her know that when she says, "Don't worry, dear," it doesn't help. Tell her you want real information and advice.

Moms want to be helpful and not hurtful. But by now you've probably realized that when you were seven and wore pink polka dot pants with a red striped shirt, your mom said, "Honey, that looks great!" That doesn't mean she lied. More likely she was encouraging your life skills of learning how to dress. Now that you're older, you can share with her how you need to hear straight talk—that you understand she loves you but that you want to hear her real opinion.

Despite your occasional doubts, your mom does know a few things. She has been around longer and can see the world from an older perspective. Imagine: how different the world would look if you were suddenly two feet shorter than you are now? Instead of looking straight out or down, you would need to look up. Your mom has vast experience in seeing things as they truly are because she is an adult.

*About 81% of 10-year-olds are afraid of being fat. Guess what? Your mom understands this fear, so talk to her about what is real and what is introduced by the media that makes everyone think they aren't skinny enough.

When chatting, ask your mom to be honest in her comments. And, in return, you can do the same. Do your part and share how you honestly feel. Listen in your "gut" for what feels right and true for you. A good way to know is if you experience a peaceful, good, or "that feels right" feeling inside.

No amount of positivity from your mom or anyone else can make you feel good if you don't believe in yourself first. See Chapter 3 on "Being Me" for more thoughts on this topic.

The Bottom Line: You are loved no matter the number on the scale. You are loved because you are YOU, not because you are skinny, chubby, or somewhere in between. Remember that your mom and other good people want to help you be your best self. Trust those helpful people and the good feeling inside that tells you this truth.

Kidspeak: "Me and my friends would always ask each other if they thought the other was skinny or not, because I always thought my mom wouldn't tell the truth. We always thought our mom was just being nice and didn't want us to feel bad about the truth. Well, really the truth wasn't bad! One day it hit me when my mom was answering my questions about weight—why would my own mom lie to me? If my mom loves me, why would she lie to her own daughter? I realized then too, that I could answer my own questions by looking in the mirror and loving my body. I know now that my mom is and will always be true to her word. And that I will never feel beautiful unless *I* truly think and feel I am beautiful."

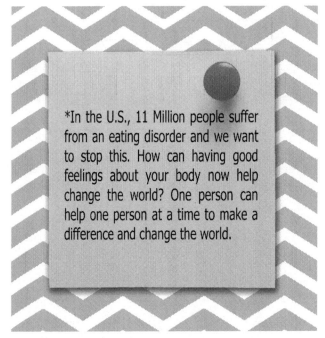

*In the U.S., 11 Million people suffer from an eating disorder and we want to stop this. How can having good feelings about your body now help change the world? One person can help one person at a time to make a difference and change the world.

SUPER SENTENCES

Being me is GREAT because

_____.

I love _____ about myself.

My top three talents are: _____, _____,

and _____.

New talents I want to develop are

_____.

I love my body because it can _____.

ONE THING I can do to be healthier [be a happier me] is

_____.

My Thoughts...

Chapter 3: Being Me

Scenario: *Lily and her sister love laughing and being silly. Lily likes to have fun and she has a lot of bubbly energy, but when she acts like this at school some of her friends look at her funny. One of her friends told her to calm down and be more serious. She noticed that another girl is bubbly like her but only around certain people. Lily wonders if maybe she should try to change herself.*

Do I need permission to be myself?

You don't need permission to be you! Be yourself and love it. Be bold and full of light and happiness about living true to yourself. You don't really need permission, but in case you're feeling like you need it, here it is! Give yourself permission to live true to your best you and embrace the amazing girl that you are.

Sometimes it's hard to feel confident in yourself at this age because it seems like everything is changing. We get it. One moment you love the carefree playing, running around, and make-believe. The next moment you wonder if you're getting to old for it. Add on the feeling of wanting to do more grown-up things. No wonder it's confusing! Other people are starting to see you as someone responsible, and you want to live up to that and do your best, but you worry that you can't do that and still be a kid. These are natural feelings that come with growing up.

Be you by cherishing these moments of childhood, who you are and what you feel, because they will soon be gone. If you live life to the fullest in the best way for this age, you'll look back with good memories and happiness.

Even if life is challenging and times get rough, the true you will sustain the joy. There will be mean girls, hard tests, changes in your body that confuse or scare you, times when you don't feel understood by your parents, friends, or *anyone*, but you will make it through. Just be you!

Today think about the person that you want to become. Think about the good traits within you and the potential that you have to change the world by touching others' lives for good. Consider these questions:

- ➢ What do you love to do?
- ➢ If you didn't have to worry about what anyone thought, what would you do?
- ➢ What are your dreams, hopes, and goals? (See more in Chapter 10 on this topic.)
- ➢ Close your eyes and think about a time when you were truly happy. Now give yourself permission to be that girl.
- ➢ You are growing and changing, but you are still the one and only amazing YOU!
- ➢ Try filling out the MY FAVES Questionnaire.

There are two ways to use the questionnaire:

One, each of you completes the questions with your own answers, then shares with the other. Choose a new topic each time it's your turn or go in order and both share your answers. OR

Two, complete the answer by guessing what the OTHER person's favorite is. Afterward, compare answers and see how close you got.

MY FAVES:

Favorite snack:

_____

Favorite family vacation:

_____

Favorite pet:

_____

Favorite fun time with Mom:

_____

Favorite movie:

_____

Favorite special treasures:

_____

Favorite book:

_____

Favorite sport:

_____

Favorite dinner:

_____

Favorite thing on a Saturday:

_____

Favorite season:

_____

Kidspeak: "One of my friends just wanted to sit and talk every recess. She said that I was too bouncy and random when I wanted to do other things. It made me feel bad and I asked my mom if maybe I was too childish. She told me that I was perfect and it was okay to be me. She told me that I have permission to be myself and maybe some of my friends didn't have that freedom. I realized that we're all different. Now I'm excited to be me because I love having fun and I'm not afraid to hang out with other girls if I get bored of sitting and talking."

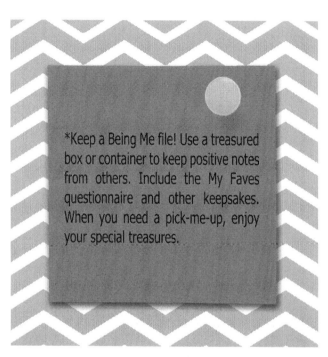

*Keep a Being Me file! Use a treasured box or container to keep positive notes from others. Include the My Faves questionnaire and other keepsakes. When you need a pick-me-up, enjoy your special treasures.

Should I be afraid to be who I am in front of other people?

No, you shouldn't be afraid to be the good person that you are. Live your life with virtue and strong values, with kindness to others, and with love for those around you, and stand up for what is right.

We all make mistakes, so it's likely you've made some, too. If you've been a "mean girl" or too bossy or rude, that's not been the true you. The good news is you can start fresh every day. If you keep trying your best and you make amends when you do make a poor choice, you'll be okay. Saying "I'm sorry," or "That wasn't helpful, let me try that again," are powerful changing phrases. They help you be the real you.

You are the smart, talented, kind, and loving girl who walks straight and tall. Don't be afraid to be that girl who lives with confidence. Sometimes you might feel like the only one willing to walk the "right" path, but take courage! Don't be afraid to be an example of someone who knows herself and behaves that way no matter what.

Your example is life-changing because it gives other girls permission to be true to themselves as well.

*Repeat to yourself: "What other people think of me is NONE of my business." People will think what they want to, you can't control that. You only control yourself. Focus on thinking good thoughts and doing good actions.

Kidspeak: "As I go throughout each day I've found that it really isn't important to please others—it's important to please myself by being me. My true, real self. I've always been really self-conscious of myself and what other people think. For example: I always put my lunch bag in front of my lunch as a cover in case anyone thought it was weird I was eating healthy. I took my mom's advice and made a decision to stop acting like this. I thought, *Everyone around here is self-conscious so if they think I'm weird, maybe they're just jealous, and they're too afraid to do what I'm doing.*

"I brought a salad to school for lunch and I was worried what people would think, but instead I thought: *It doesn't matter what they think, it doesn't change the fact that I'm eating a salad. I'll still be friends with them.* So stop being self-conscious. It doesn't make you feel good about yourself. Being yourself does!"

Can I make a difference? Am I important?

Here's a question we've seen from many girls just like you.

Can I make a difference? Am I important?

The answer is YES!

You are important and you can make a difference by celebrating and sharing the amazing gift of YOU!

The power is in you to change the world by loving yourself, being a

Children can change the world. For example, at the age of 13 Jayden Bledsoe started an IT company which by age 15 he had turned into a $3.5 million global company. A seven-year-old boy found out African children had to walk miles for water and built a well in a Ugandan village. A 13-year-old boy wrote a New York Times Bestseller on how kids can do big things.
http://t.today.com/books/boy-13-writes-nyt-bestseller-how-kids-can-do-big-2D12186988

true friend, and helping others to recognize the truth in the secrets you've learned in this book.

One person can make a difference. One smile can make a difference. Decide today to make a positive change that will light up the world with goodness.

> ➢ Be happy about who you are and celebrate this incredible journey of growing into a powerful young lady.
> ➢ Smile at 10 people today.
> ➢ Include a new friend in your group. Seek out someone who looks like they could use some friendship and invite them to play at recess.
> ➢ Choose one habit to change in your life to be healthier. (See Chapter 1 for more ideas.)
> ➢ Take 10 minutes today to do something silly or enjoyable.
> ➢ Share this book with someone.

Kidspeak: "By being me I can make a difference. Even if it is small, it is still a difference. I love the quote by Elaine Dalton, 'If you want to make a difference in the world, you have to be different from the world.' I have this hanging up in my room. I believe that people make the difference in the world and that I can be that difference in others."

SUPER SENTENCES

My unique personality is great because

_____

I can make a difference by

_____.

People say they love this about me:

_____.

When someone makes me feel badly for being me, I can say

_____.

ONE THING that helps me be my BEST ME is

_____.

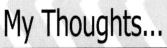

My Thoughts...

Chapter 4: Mom and Me

Scenario: *You've been looking forward to going to a movie with friends on Saturday. But when you tell your mom what movie you're planning to see, she says it's not appropriate for your age. She also reminds you that it's family game night. At first, you're angry. You've already made other plans! And, though you love your mom and family game night, it's important to you to spend time with friends today. What do you do?*

Why do I fight more with my mom? Does she not love me as much?

As mothers, both authors have a total of five daughters who are growing and maturing just like you. So we can tell you, from real experience, that your mother loves you very much, even if you argue! At this stage, you may experience more disagreements because you are growing up and things are changing. Feelings are changing from moment to moment. It can be hard to understand what's happening with your body, your emotions, and the emotions of the people around you. You're outgrowing your "child" skin and growing into a more mature "young woman" skin. This means adjustments!

A few key things can help with the transition. Showing respect to your parents or other adults is important to being treated as a grown-up yourself. It's hard to be seen as older if you talk rudely, act moody or sulky, or have a tantrum because of not getting your way.

Show love to your mom. This is a big adjustment for her, too. Don't be afraid to ask questions. Talk about how your body is changing. Share what you're thinking, your fears, worries, and excitement. Ask your mom to just listen. She might be worrying about things just like you and can use the chat time to feel connected with you. Use this book to help give you ideas on talking through your questions. There's a section just for moms to help with this very situation.

Think on what you're arguing about. Maybe it's about rules or boundaries that your mom has set. It's okay to feel differently—share those feelings in a kind, clear way. Ask your mom to explain the rules so you understand. Discuss compromises or other ways to choose the best solution. Until you can find the right fit, show respect to your mom by continuing to follow the rule. This builds trust between you and your mom. The more your parents trust your choices and ability to see their point of view, the more freedom they can give.

As you learn to express yourself and talk about your feelings, the relationship between you and your parents will be strengthened. Remember that even though you feel older, you're still a sixth-grader. Many growing years are ahead of you with so much to learn. Give your mom an extra chance and try to look at things from her perspective. Try hard to understand each other and think the best. It will make each day easier and more joyful.

Give your mom a hug. Tell her that you love her and appreciate her. Arguments will happen, but there's always a chance to forgive and make things better. Saying sorry or making a funny experience from a negative one creates connection and trust.

Kidspeak: "I've noticed more frustration at times, and to me, it's all normal. If you and your mom are both going through hormone things and if you argue, it's okay. All families argue. It's not so much fighting, just a little bit of a heated debate. If you fight with your mom on a daily basis, talk to her and express your feelings. That way you both get a good connection between you and your mom. And you can even try to find coping skills. What I do when I get heated is I go outside for a run. At night I go into a place where I am alone and where no one can bother me. So that's what I think is the best thing to do when a heated debate goes on with you and your mom. Exchange feelings and find coping skills."

I want to be with my friends more than my mom. Is that bad?

Creating and enjoying great friendships is part of being a kid and growing up. As you get older, you might find that you have more interests in common with your friends than you knew before. It's normal and okay at this age to want to hang out with your friends more.

At the same time, it's important to respect when your mom wants you to take part in family activities. What do you do in the scenario above?

First, your concern shows that you're a wonderful daughter. You're thinking about how this will affect your mom. Second, talk respectfully with her about it. Share that you love being with her and the family and explain that you had made these plans first. Try to find a compromise—can you skip this one time but be sure to come the next? Can you choose a different movie that is more age appropriate for you and your friends to watch?

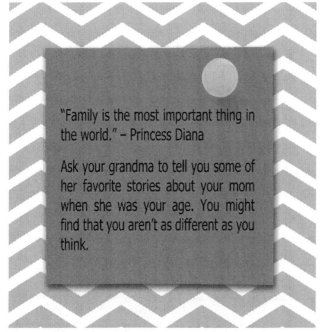

"Family is the most important thing in the world." – Princess Diana

Ask your grandma to tell you some of her favorite stories about your mom when she was your age. You might find that you aren't as different as you think.

However, if your mom says you need to participate with the family, then go with a great attitude and be happy to make a memory. Remember that in only six or seven years, you'll be on your own at college or working. Time you spend with family now will be more appreciated then.

As much as possible, decide with your mom how much time you get to spend with friends as well as family. In Connie's home our kids can have playdates on Wednesday, Friday, and Saturday. We plan the week in advance to avoid problems. Ask your mom what's a reasonable schedule to create a healthy mix of friend and family time.

*Spending time with your family can be simple and fun: play board games, pop some popcorn, play tag or hide-n-seek, eat dinner

together, make a fun dessert, do an impromptu talent show, have each person share a high or low about the day.

Kidspeak: "When you reach this age you want to be more social, be with friends and with a group. Don't spend all your time with friends, you do need to have family time. Like this Saturday, my friends and I are having a party. But on Friday, I'm going shopping with my Mom. That way I get to spend time with both my mom and my friends. Try to balance that time with each one."

SUPER SENTENCES

I know my Mom loves me because

_____.

I can show my Mom I love her by

_____.

I like to spend time with friends doing

_____.

Instead of getting angry at my Mom, I can

_____.

I can use respectful words and phrases with my Mom like

_____.

My Thoughts...

Chapter 5: Puberty

Scenario: *Alyssa went to the pool with her friends and was so excited to go swimming. When she started changing into her swimsuit she noticed that her period had started. She felt a little worried until she remembered that her mom had helped her prepare a "personal pouch" tucked safely into her bag with supplies that she needed. Alyssa noticed that the locker room at the pool also had a vending machine with tampons for people to buy. Her period wasn't a problem after all.*

When I have my period, will people still like me? Will I still be me? What if I start my period away from home?

Here's the thing: when you have your period no one will know that anything has changed unless you tell them. There is no outward physical change that occurs when a girl has her period. You are still you! You are still the thoughtful individual that is recognizing herself and the changes in your life with a positive attitude.

Getting your period is just another stepping stone along the path of growing up. Things change and that is often hard to understand or deal with, but please know that every woman in the world goes through puberty, has a period, and grows through maturation. It's a beautiful time of your life to experience.

If you're not comfortable talking about this with your friends, you don't have to tell them. It's your body and this is a private thing that you shouldn't feel pressured to talk about. That being said, if you do want to talk to your friends about your period and they are comfortable with it, then it's okay. Just remember that young girls often don't completely understand everything there is to know about the body and changes that occur in maturation. Your friends might share incorrect information or say things that make you scared or worried because they aren't explaining correctly. If you have questions or hear something that doesn't seem right or doesn't make sense, don't hesitate to ask your parents or guardian.

Questions are wonderful things because they lead you to answers. Don't be shy about asking enough questions to understand what is happening with your body. Both your mom and dad can help you with questions about your period and it's totally okay to talk about. Together, you can visit health sites like WebMD.com to find out more specifics.

You may be worried that you won't know when you will start your period. Most likely you will have signs leading up to it, like a bit of light spotting of blood right before. The spots may be a water-color pink or small spots of red. Usually it's light enough you can take care of it without anyone else being aware of it.

If you aren't at home when your period starts, that could make you understandably nervous. The best way to get over fears is to be prepared. Something as simple as putting a panty liner or pad in a zippered pocket of your backpack will help. Many of these products come individually wrapped in tiny packages that can be hidden in your bag for future use. Ask your mom for help and even create a "personal pouch" to keep in your backpack that has a change of underwear, prepackaged wet wipe, pad, and panty liner.

If you're at school and you're not prepared, don't worry. The school nurse will have supplies for you to use. Just go to the office and politely ask for help. No need to feel hesitant—nurses don't get embarrassed about anything!

What if you're not at school or home? Even though it may be awkward, ask a friend to help get supplies. Your friend's mom or any adult woman has definitely gone through all the changes of maturation and would be happy to help. If you're in a public place, most restrooms have a place where you can purchase a pad or tampon with change—usually only a quarter up to one dollar.

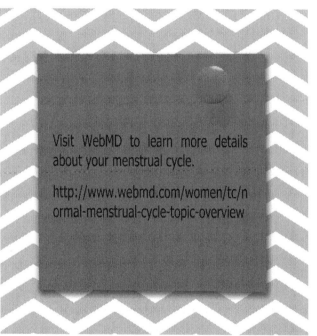

Visit WebMD to learn more details about your menstrual cycle.

http://www.webmd.com/women/tc/normal-menstrual-cycle-topic-overview

Kidspeak: "People will still like you because this is just a part of life. If it happens away from home, don't worry. One day I went to the store with my mom and while we were both in different places getting things, I felt this whoosh of something wet. I went to the bathroom immediately to see what it was. When I checked, it was a clear wet discharge with a speck of what looked like blood. I felt worried. I went immediately and told my mom and she said, 'Don't worry, it's not the real thing. This is normal to happen before your period starts. We can go home and get some new clothes and a pad.' So we did. She gave me an extra pad to take to school and asked me to call her if anything more happened. It didn't. I felt calm and relaxed at what she said. And I felt like this was an easy thing to take care of. If it happens again, now I know what to do."

I feel emotional for no reason. Am I being a baby?

Hormones are tiny chemicals inside our brain that can create BIG changes in our body. One of those changes is how you experience emotions. The hormones being released do make you feel different. At times you'll be tired, sad, angry, or irritable. You could also feel excited, happy, and energized. And often for no reason at all! This is normal. When you can recognize the emotional shifts, you can choose a wise response.

Take time to listen to your body. If you're tired, ask yourself if you're getting enough sleep. Did you know that sixth- and seventh-graders are supposed to get nine to ten hours of sleep a night? Being overtired can make any emotion more dramatic and intense.

The levels of hormones being released will fluctuate throughout your cycle each month. This process starts before you get your period. Sometimes you might feel like you want to cry about everything. Other times you'd like to shout for joy. And sometimes you just feel downright mad. By taking good care of yourself, you can help even out the fluctuations in your body.

> ➢ Exercise every day. Do something fun that you enjoy. It could be walking, dancing, playing a sport or tag, doing gymnastics or cheer, or anything else that will get you up and moving.
>
> ➢ Notice how exercising makes you feel more alert, alive, and aware of your body.

If you feel extremely emotional, you aren't being a baby. Even though it doesn't feel natural, this is a natural part of the changes your body is going through. Don't be afraid to talk to your mom or dad about how you feel. Oftentimes simply telling someone about it helps a lot, because you name the problem and realize it's normal. Don't be too hard on yourself if your emotions are a bit out of control. Be aware of yourself and this reminder: **My emotions are a part of me, but I can choose my response.** Do something to feel calm again, like listening to soothing music or reading a good book.

> ➢ Change things up. Don't get caught in a slump when you're feeling emotional. Do something different.
>
> ➢ Find someone you can help and reach out to them. The best medicine for a mopey attitude is to serve someone else.
>
> ➢ Keep a journal. Start by using the journal pages included in this book.
>
> ➢ Go to www.coachmom.org and download our Super Sentence Cards. Create your affirmations and use those to remind you of the great things in your life.

Writing feelings in a journal helps clear emotional baggage. And when you look back at your journal from time to time, it will help you to see how you're doing and to spot familiar patterns of behaving. Sometimes it might surprise you just how strong, smart, and incredible you have always been.

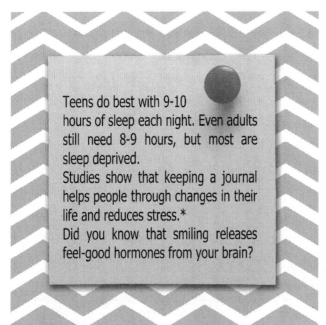

Teens do best with 9-10 hours of sleep each night. Even adults still need 8-9 hours, but most are sleep deprived.
Studies show that keeping a journal helps people through changes in their life and reduces stress.*
Did you know that smiling releases feel-good hormones from your brain?

Kidspeak: "I've learned a lot about this one. First, it's okay, because this is what you go through. Your mom and dad will understand. If you get emotional, find coping skills and ways to fight the anger. Some of the coping skills I use are to go outside and go for a run or a jog, do something physical; go into an unoccupied room to calm down; or use words to share my feelings, like 'I'm angry right now, I need to go cool off' or 'This really frustrates me when…' That helps your parents know how you're feeling, and helps you control your emotions."

My body is doing some weird things. Is that normal?

Parts of puberty can feel a little strange. Suddenly you're growing hair in new places and sweating more than ever. Is this normal? Perfectly! Noticing those changes means that your body is functioning as it should and that you are growing up.

The process of maturing changes several things in the body. Although it may seem odd, these changes make your body more efficient and prepared for the future. Let's talk about a few of these changes.

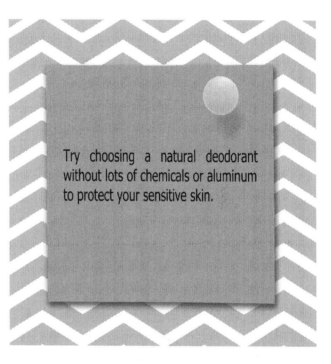

Try choosing a natural deodorant without lots of chemicals or aluminum to protect your sensitive skin.

Hair. Yes, you will have hair that grows under your armpits and around your pubic area or vagina. Usually it's just a bit at first. Most likely you won't need to shave under your arms for a few more years. Be sure and check with your parent before you start doing that so that you don't damage the delicate skin under your arms.

You'll also notice that your hair starts to look oily or greasy after just a few days. This is all normal. Your body starts to produce more oils in response to different hormones in your body. Shower or bathe regularly but don't shampoo your hair every day. Doing that can actually dry out your scalp and then make your body start to produce more oils to compensate. Many hair experts recommend shampooing every other day or every third day to keep a natural level of oils in the hair. You will have to take note of what works for your own hair. If it's really thick, you can go longer without washing, whereas if you have finer, thinner hair, you might need to wash it more often. There are also lots of great hair care products that help you care for healthy hair. Check with your mom and read the recommendations in Chapter 1 on Beauty & Body Image for more information.

Along with oils in your hair, your body will start to produce a bit of discharge. You might notice a little yellow in your underwear and

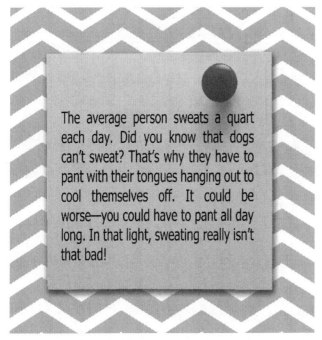

The average person sweats a quart each day. Did you know that dogs can't sweat? That's why they have to pant with their tongues hanging out to cool themselves off. It could be worse—you could have to pant all day long. In that light, sweating really isn't that bad!

this is also normal. This is something that comes before you start your period. Most girls will start to notice a little discharge two to three years before their first period. Change your underwear each day and keep your personal areas clean.

Another part of puberty is sweat. Yuck, right? Well, this is normal, too, and actually, sweating is a pretty miraculous thing that our body does to protect us. Sweating keeps our body at the right temperature and also rids the body of some toxins. It's okay to sweat, just be sure to wear deodorant and shower regularly. That means you could take a shower every day or at least every other day in the sixth grade. Have fun choosing a deodorant that makes you feel clean and happy. There are dozens of scents and perfumed deodorants and soaps available. Keeping your body clean is important. If you feel uncomfortable or itchy, check with your mom to make sure you aren't having any reactions to deodorants or soaps.

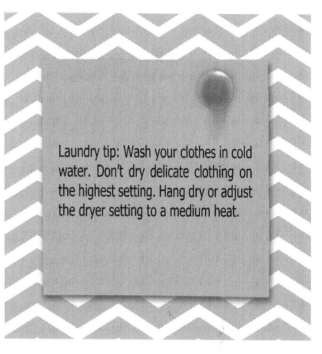

Laundry tip: Wash your clothes in cold water. Don't dry delicate clothing on the highest setting. Hang dry or adjust the dryer setting to a medium heat.

Wear clean clothes and ask your mom to teach you how to do laundry so that you can help out. If you sweat a lot, try using stain remover on the armpits of your shirts. Learning to take care of your clothes is part of growing up. Show your parents how responsible you can be!

Kidspeak: "I didn't realize that my body wouldn't change all at once. It actually takes a few years for all of the different changes to happen. I talked with my mom and it made me feel better that I really am normal. Now I don't feel so nervous and it's actually fun to wear good smelling deodorant!"

Some girls are developing faster than I am, is there something wrong with me?

Rachelle's family has a beautiful peach tree in their backyard, and every year they anticipate the time when they can pick ripe, delicious peaches the size of softballs and eat them with sweet juices running down their chins. Each year about two weeks ahead of picking time, you can find peaches that are ready to eat. Ironically, at times you'll see peaches on the same tree in different stages of ripeness: some fruit is ready to pick, some peaches are still green and hard, and others are in between—neither ripe nor green.

What does puberty have to do with peaches? Well, each one of you are like a peach on the tree, growing and maturing at your own rate. Yes, most of our peaches are ripe about the same time, but there are large bunches of early and late peaches. Just as your body is unique, so is the process of maturation.

You may have heard people reference puberty and maturation as having something to do with a biological clock. If you were to run around your house right now, I bet you'd find that each of your clocks would state a different time. The clock in your bedroom might be two minutes earlier than the clock in the living room and the clock in the bathroom might be one minute later. This doesn't mean there is something wrong with the clock in your bedroom. It was just set at a different time. So it is keeping time just like a clock should, but on its own schedule.

Your body does have a biological clock and it moves on its own schedule. You might notice that some of your friends are talking about their period starting and yours hasn't yet. That is totally okay. Puberty can start as early as age 8 and as late as age 13—that's a five-year difference! There is nothing wrong with you and the rate at which your body matures.

Remember peaches and puberty. You can't force a peach to be ready before its time. With patience, the peach and your body will grow into something magnificent.

When you think about all that goes into growing a human body—the systems, hormones, timing, and more—it's incredible so many of us grow correctly at all! Try not to compare yourself to others because they each have their own personal clock set at the right time for their body.

Kidspeak: "I know that no one has the same body I do and everyone's works differently. My mom has talked to me before about all of us growing differently and now I understand that we all have our own times to develop."

SUPER SENTENCES:

I know my body is shifting and THAT IS GREAT!

I feel_____ because_____ ,

but I would prefer_____.

One way I can appreciate my body is

_____.

I can control my emotions by

_____.

My Thoughts...

Chapter 6: Boys

Scenario: *Trisha checked her email and found a note from Chad, a boy in her class, asking her to "go out" with him. Chad was nice and fun to be around, and Trisha thought his blue eyes were cute, but she wasn't sure what to do. She talked to her mom and together they decided something that felt good to Trisha. She emailed Chad and told him that she really wanted to be his friend and maybe they could play basketball at school with their other friends.*

Am I supposed to be dating or in a relationship with a boy at my age?

It might sound like fun to have a boyfriend at your age. Your friends may talk about having one or about how someone texted a boy and he now calls her a girlfriend. At this age, it's normal for girls to like boys, but it's a little early to be dating, having boyfriends, or getting too serious with a boy.

What does that mean? Well, think about all that we've discussed in this little book about growing up. Your body is changing, going through puberty, and experiencing all kinds of hormones, emotions, etc. There is so much change. Right now is not the time to be dating. It's a time for growing up and learning more about you. It's a time to enjoy being you without the pressure of a boyfriend.

Talk to your parents about setting rules together to be prepared for this important time in your life. Many experts recommend waiting until age sixteen to date, and that's a wise starting point. Discuss what is appropriate as far as texting, calling, and emailing boys. You shouldn't be holding hands, kissing a boy, or spending time alone with him at this age.

Firm rules make it easier for you to be prepared so that things don't get out of hand. And they give you a ready response for when you're in a situation with a boy.

Kidspeak: "It's okay to have a little crush, but not be boyfriend-girlfriend. It's not helpful when some boys like to lean in, go on dates, or have a first kiss, which ruins the friendship. Enjoy having a little crush and leave it at that. My teacher's fiancé actually proposed to her in front of the class. It made sense because she's twenty-four and ready to get married. We're in sixth-grade. We should not be in deep relationships!"

If a boy doesn't like me, does that mean I'm not pretty? How can I get a boy to like me?

If a boy doesn't like you, that simply means he is normal. Boys go through puberty a few years later than girls and as a result, they aren't as interested in girls in sixth grade. Most boys are more interested in sports, excelling in school, and outdoor activities. Even if they do kind of like a girl, they often don't feel like showing it because they don't want to be teased by other kids.

Sure, having attention from boys is kind of fun. However, staying just friends makes life a whole lot happier. He will see you as a person—a talented girl with many wonderful personality traits—not just for the way your hair or body looks. In fact, when asked, many sixth-grade boys shared that they liked a girl who was fun, happy, smart, and not annoying. Looks didn't even make the cut. If a boy likes you only because you're pretty, he isn't the boy for you.

So what should you do if a boy asks you to be his girlfriend? Or to "go out" with him?

As long as you're not going out on a date, it's okay to be friends with a boy. If it's okay with your parents, you can talk to each other and possibly share how you feel—that you'd like to be good friends.

Many kids are carrying on conversations through the internet and phones with each other. This is different than how your parents experienced having a crush on a boy or a girl. When we authors were in fifth and sixth grade, if we liked a boy, we might write them a note or have a friend talk to them. It didn't go much past that.

Fast forward to your time. Now it's so easy to "pass notes" via text and other methods. There's nothing wrong with this until things go overboard. The tricky part is that there are so many ways to communicate that aren't face to face or real-time, things can get out of hand.

How do things go overboard or get out of hand? Here's something that will help you determine what we mean.

When you are texting, emailing, or instant messaging a boy—or *anyone* for that matter—ask yourself this question: *Would I say this to his face? If he were in this room with me right now, would I say what I am typing?*

If that makes you feel uncomfortable then you need to tone it down. It's easy to get serious over email and texting because you'll say things that are somewhat embarrassing. Since no one can see your face, it makes you have a false sense of confidence. The natural feelings you have to like a boy are okay. Keeping communication to "friendship words" is ideal.

Sometimes girls start liking a boy and communicating with him via text or email and things get serious too fast. What happens after a few weeks of texting? What happens when one or the other of you get tired

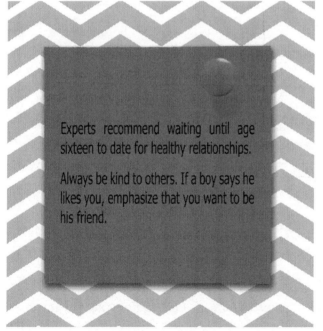

Experts recommend waiting until age sixteen to date for healthy relationships.

Always be kind to others. If a boy says he likes you, emphasize that you want to be his friend.

of this early form of a relationship? One word: awkward.

You want to be able to feel good about yourself and how you acted. Think about how much longer you'll still be going to school with this boy. Most likely it will be about five to six more years. You want to be good friends and not say or do anything that would cause you to feel uncomfortable or embarrassed down the road.

Don't worry about boys liking you at this age. Stop worrying about having a boyfriend or if you're pretty enough for a boy. Instead focus on creating great friendships.

The quick tip is to remember that even though you may feel like you're old enough for a boyfriend, you are not. Enjoy this wonderful time of your life, the freedom to enjoy your childhood, creating friendships, and discovering yourself.

Kidspeak: "If a boy doesn't like you it doesn't mean you're not pretty at all. At this age, boys are looking for the show-off 'girly girls.' But that doesn't mean you have to change your looks. Just be who you are and don't worry about it at this age. It's always good to look your best. But don't overdo it. Girls can put on tons of makeup and focus on their hair just to be liked. And it makes them look weird. Be yourself. Look your best. And like yourself."

Why do boys try to act like they're all that and a bag of chips? Why are they annoying or aggressive?

Boys are going through changes just like you. It may seem weird to think about, but boys are starting to have hormones, emotions, and other changes in their bodies, too. This might make them feel uncertain about how to act around girls. They are working out transitions with school, friendships, and a curious interest in girls.

Some boys might tease to get your attention. That doesn't necessarily mean they like you, but they do want attention. Other boys might do silly things to show off for their friends. Most boys feel a bit nervous around girls because they notice that you are changing and growing up and they aren't sure how to act.

That is not to say that unacceptable behavior is okay. A boy should never be disrespectful to a girl. Boys tend to get physical with each other when they are playing, like shoving or hitting each other, even wrestling. A boy should never shove you or get physical with you. If he does, tell him to stop. If he says, "I'm just kidding," then you need to tell him, "That is not okay with me. I'm a girl and you need to treat me with respect."

You can help out your boy classmates by telling them, "Hey, I'd like to be your friend, but when you tease me it's not fun." And remember that if you don't want them acting out around you, you'll have to check yourself and make sure you aren't teasing and bugging them right back.

If you have troubles with a boy annoying you, pressuring you to do something you don't want to do, or otherwise making you feel uncomfortable, even after you ask him to stop, talk to an adult and ask for help. Your teacher, parent, principal, or guardian should help you. Make sure that they understand how you feel and that you want them to help you.

Kidspeak: "Boys act like that to impress girls. They think that being annoying or doing crazy extreme stunts will impress, when it actually makes the girls not like them. They try to be muscular and look and be cool. Handle it by telling the boy directly, 'Knock it off,' or 'Be yourself.' Pay more attention to the guys who are kinder, gentler, and not show-offs."

SUPER SENTENCES

I get healthy attention from others by

_____.

If a boy is annoying me I can

_____.

When I feel others are prettier, I remember

_____.

I like to focus on my talents of

_____.

I can stay friends with boys by

_____.

My Thoughts...

Chapter 7: Friends

"Kindred spirits are not so scarce as I used to think. It's splendid to find out there are so many of them in the world."

—L.M. Montgomery, *Anne of Green Gables*

Scenario: *Carly wore a pink shirt with lace on the sleeves and Tracy told her it looked like a baby shirt. Anna disagreed and said that she loved Carly's shirt. Tracy told them they were both dumb and needed to get some real style. How could Carly and Anna respond to Tracy?*

How do I find true friends?

In this time of your life, it's great to have lots of friends. Most likely, you have several friends—a few fun ones and maybe a BFF or two. Occasionally, you might wonder to yourself

Good friends are like stars, you don't have to see them to know they're always there.

if the girl you've been hanging out with is a true friend, because at times she makes you feel uncomfortable. Maybe you're fighting about dumb things, or maybe she is telling you that you can't be friends with someone else or shouldn't wear certain clothing, etc.

It might help to remember that everyone has a bad day now and then and can act snotty or rude. But if that friend continues to act inappropriately and you don't feel good when you are around her, then she is not being a true friend.

Let's talk about some characteristics of a true friend.

A T.R.U.E. friend is

Trustworthy and always honest

Respectful and helps you keep your standards

Understanding of who you are and never tries to make you be someone you aren't

Excited to be your friend in any situation

> ➤ A true friend is someone who loves you for who you are. A true friend would not say, "If you don't wear your hair like this, I won't be your friend anymore."

> ➤ A true friend would not pressure you to do something that lowers your standards. A true friend respects you and wants to help you be the best person you can be.

> ➤ A true friend is fun to be around.

> ➤ A true friend understands what real friendship is and that girls have changing feelings. A true friend realizes that everyone makes mistakes but there is always room for forgiveness.

We've talked about what a true friend is, so how do you find true friends?

You probably already have some true friends, so first, be aware of and cherish them! To find more friends, look for that person who is consistently kind, happy, and supportive of you being your best self. Do you have a friend that you love to laugh with? That is another quality that is wonderful to have in a friendship. What about a friend who cheers you on when you do something great and can be there for you when you're feeling down?

The best way to find a true friend is to BE a true friend. Look back at the list of qualities we've discussed and challenge yourself to be a true friend. When you are playing with your friends, make a point to be trustworthy, respectful, understanding, and excited.

Kidspeak: "I know who my true friends are because they are the ones who I can be myself around. If I were to make a mistake, I know my friends would forgive me and forget about it."

Should I try to make everyone else happy all the time?

You should try to be a true friend, but everyone else's happiness is not your responsibility. Yes, we can be a great influence and help lighten someone's day, but ultimately the decision to be happy lies within each one of us.

The problem with someone who continually acts sad or complains about themselves is that their actions drain your energy. It can be like someone turning off all the lights in a room, leaving you with a dim and yucky feeling. That is no fun!

If you have a friend who is constantly unhappy and looking for you to fix the situation by giving her endless praise and being her personal cheerleader, then it might be time to put some space between you and that girl. Everyone has some down days and friends are meant to encourage each other. But you don't need to be unhappy in a friendship. You are not responsible to

A true friend helps you be a better person than you were before you knew them.
—Coach Mom

make someone else be happy all the time.

Now, occasionally children can have a real problem with depression. If you are worried about your friend, please talk to your school counselor, your parents, or even your friend's parents.

An eighth-grade girl I know (we'll call her Katie) had a good friend who seemed kind of down and wasn't her normal self. Then Katie noticed that her friend had some scratches or cut marks on her arms and wrists. When Katie asked her friend about the cuts, she said it was nothing. Katie was worried about her friend, so when she got home from school, she called her friend's mom to talk about it. That mother was so grateful and was able to have a good talk with the friend to figure out the situation. Katie's friend was upset at first, but later she was glad that Katie cared enough to do something brave for a friend in need.

Remember what makes a T.R.U.E. Friend. To have a friend you must be a friend first.

It's important to think about your friendship in healthy terms. A healthy friendship is one where both friends care about each other and each take turns being the sunshine. Be kind to everyone and be a good friend, but let others take responsibility for their own happiness.

Kidspeak: "I like to make other people happy but I don't feel like I have to *make* them happy. If they asked me to do something that I didn't agree with, I wouldn't do it just to make them happy. It isn't worth sacrificing my own happiness for theirs. Sometimes what they think will bring them happiness will not make them truly happy."

How do I disagree with my friends? Will they hate me?

We're all created to have a unique sense of our own self. That means that we think differently and have various opinions. Sometimes we want to do something fun that someone else thinks is weird. Guess what? That's okay.

Disagreeing is a normal part of life. It doesn't have to be a negative thing, though. It's perfectly acceptable to have different opinions, but we should always be kind in expressing them.

Maybe you love gymnastics but your friend says it's dumb and that everyone should play basketball. It's okay to disagree, but not okay to tell someone their interest is dumb just because it's different.

So what if you want to play soccer and your friend would rather shoot hoops at recess? Politely tell your friend how you feel. Be fair and see if you can meet each other halfway.

"I'd really like to play soccer today. Since we played basketball yesterday, would you mind playing soccer today?" Hopefully, your friend will be okay with this idea, but there's a good chance that maybe she won't. If not, just say, "Okay, I'm going to play soccer anyway because I really need a break from basketball. Thanks for understanding."

Will your friend hate you if you disagree or want to do something different? She may be upset but that's okay. Let her work out the frustration in her way. If your friend is being rude or threatening by saying, "Well, I won't be your friend anymore," don't respond by giving in. Instead, try something like this: "I'm sorry you feel that way. I'd still like to be your friend, but maybe we need to take a break from each other today."

The truth of the matter is what we discussed earlier about being a true friend. A true friend won't try to manipulate or force you to do something you don't want to do. A true friend would not threaten a friendship over something as simple as basketball.

What if it's something a lot more serious than basketball? Maybe your friend is going to meet a boy for a date without her parents knowing and wants you to come along. The same guidelines apply. Do what you know is right. Respectfully and clearly state: "I don't want to do that." Then act on it.

Between friends there will be lots of disagreements about little things, like the best singer, sports star, school, or even style of clothing. It's okay to disagree as long as you are kind.

Kidspeak: "I can disagree with friends, but it depends on the friend. If you have a friend that's bossier and forces people to do what they want, you have to set a limit. I know what it's like to have a bossy friend and to make choices I didn't really want to just make her happy. But I told her I needed a break, and I started making new friends. In doing that, I've made better friendships and I'm happier. Sometimes it's okay to disagree, because we all have our different opinions. And good friends respect different opinions. But you should not be made to feel bad about not agreeing. Or made to feel you have to do what they want in order for them to be happy or to like you. It's all about the strength of the friendship."

Kidspeak: "One time my friends and I were sharing opinions on orcas and if they were mindless killing machines or gentle, misunderstood creatures. The conversation got a speck heated! But then I said, 'Is there anything wrong with my opinion on the orcas?' And my friends replied, 'No, there's nothing wrong at all!' It felt great to know that my friends understood my opinion and that I have a different love for these creatures."

SUPER SENTENCES:

I don't have to make others happy. By **being happy**, I make the world a happier place!

When friends disagree I can say

_____.

One way I can be a true friend is to

_____.

When others gossip, I can reply with

_____.

One way I can share my feelings with friends is to say, I feel

_____ about _____.

My Thoughts...

Chapter 8: Peer Pressure

Scenario: *Every day the "popular" people sit together at lunch. You sit with a few trusted friends, but you still feel left out of the main group. Sometimes you hear them talking about other girls and laughing. They aren't always nice, yet you still kind of wish you were part of the group. What is it about being "popular" that you don't understand?*

Should I believe the mean things others say about me?

Let's talk for a minute about why people say mean things about others. Most of the time when kids are being mean, rude, or disrespectful, it comes from a lack of personal balance or a difficulty in dealing with life issues. Some kids are hurting inside, so they lash out. Others point a finger at someone else hoping their own "flaws" won't be noticed. Some suffer serious problems at home that make it hard to concentrate in school, and some simply have no good role models to teach them how to act and treat others.

Some kids tend to gossip—that means saying unkind, untrue, or even unkind but true things about someone else. Remember, just because something is true doesn't mean it should be shared. Gossip hurts. And when more intense, gossip can become bullying. If you're in a conversation and girls say phrases like "Did you hear about..." or "I don't like her because I heard she..." then you know it's gossip. You can be brave and respond with phrases like "I don't feel good talking like that about someone," or "I don't want to talk about someone be-hind their back. Let's ask her." When people who gossip are challenged to talk to the person they're talking about, they will often stop.

If girls are talking meanly about you, there are several choices in how to respond. The obvious first choice is to simply ignore it. Go on your merry way doing good, being kind, and living happily. At first this may seem hard, but it gets easier over time, especially when you realize how often gossipers talk and it amounts to nothing.

Another choice is to approach the person in private, repeat what you heard, and ask if they said it. Often the person will deny it, even if it's true. But again, confrontation creates awareness, and that could help stop the problem. Simply say, "I would appreciate it if you didn't speak unkindly about me." Then do your own thing and let it go.

Lastly, if the gossiping continues or escalates, tell your mom or a trusted teacher or school authority. Your example will strengthen other kids who aren't as brave. And it will tell the gossipers or bullies that their behavior won't be tolerated.

There are many excellent resources to learn more about how to stop bullying and stay safe. Here's one of them: http://pbskids.org/itsmylife/friends/bullies/

Another reason some kids act mean is that they come from broken or abusive homes. There are many kinds of abuse: mental, verbal, drug, alcohol, and even physical abuse. Beyond that, some kids aren't sure where they'll get their next meal. Imagine how hungry you are when you come home from school. Now imagine opening the fridge and the cupboards to find nothing but a few stale crackers and a can of beans. This is the reality for many kids.

Those who lack proper nutrition, lack a secure home life, or suffer from abuse have a rougher time in life. Many of these kids choose to rise above their situations, which means they are still kind, work hard in school, and try to do what's right. Other kids, unfortunately, act out, sometimes try to abuse others, and cause problems in social settings such as school.

Hopefully this helps paint a picture for you to see how others kids might feel. It might answer the question of what is going on in their heads that influences them to act in such negative ways. But it doesn't make the behavior okay. You still need to talk with the person directly, tell them  to stop, or confide in your mom or a trusted adult. Poor behavior has a better chance of changing when someone says, "Stop."

- A note from Coach Mom if you need help:

If you're reading this and I've just described your home life, there are wonderful programs that can help both you and your family. Visit coachmom.org or this website, http://www.feedingamerica.org/take-action/advocate/federal-hunger-relief-programs/, to learn more about programs that can help you. It is okay to ask for help. No child should ever go hungry, and if you live in the United States of America there are plenty of programs to help hungry kids. There is even a toll free number that you can call, the National Child Abuse Hotline: 1-800-422-4453. https://www.childhelp.org/hotline/

Kidspeak: "When I read this it made me understand and look at things differently. It made me feel so grateful to have a roof over my head, food in the fridge, a warm bed to sleep in, and best of all a stay-at-home mom who takes care of me! Instead of fighting back or be-lieving what these kids say, I think it would be better to try to feel what they are feeling and to understand as if you were in their shoes. I think you would be a better person if you looked at them and listened and tried to understand and help."

Who makes "popular groups" popular?

This is an excellent question and one not easily answered because of many variables. Sometimes a new kid becomes popular because they are new and different. Sometimes a bully is popular because people are scared to stand up to that person. Other times popular people are simply those who are funny, easy going, or accepting of others.

But right now, you might be wondering why you, or anyone, can't simply walk up and be part of the "popular" group. Maybe you are feel-ing left out or that those kids are mean or snobs. The great thing is that you are in control. If you think a group of people is popular, then that is how you have defined them. If instead, you look at a group of people as simply that—people who are each unique and different, like you—things change.

We challenge you to look at the situation differently. Maybe you haven't given those girls a chance to be your friend because you felt they were out of reach. Perhaps you don't seem to have anything in common with them. Or you may be looking for acceptance outside of yourself and what you know to be good.

A good question to ask yourself is, are they the type of girls you *want* to be friends with? Yes, popular groups exist. But before you change yourself to fit in that group, let's talk about how girls are sometimes like chickens.

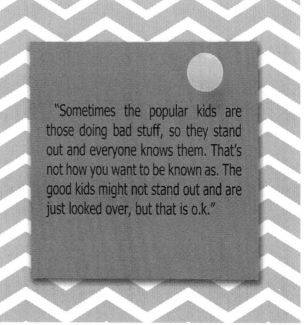

"Sometimes the popular kids are those doing bad stuff, so they stand out and everyone knows them. That's not how you want to be known as. The good kids might not stand out and are just looked over, but that is o.k."

Did you know that even chickens pick on each other and pick a "popular" hen? It's called the "pecking order," and scientists have studied this phenomenon with much fascination because a lot of pre-teen and teenage girls and boys act similar to chickens.

For some reason, one of the chickens decides that she is the boss. If you've ever heard the saying, "She rules the roost," you'll understand where that expression comes from. It comes from hens in a roost where one is the dominant ruler over the other hens. Often these hens can be downright mean, pecking other hens, plucking out feathers, damaging eggs, and even in severe cases pecking another chicken to death.

I want you to imagine the horror of one chicken pecking another and then the rest of the chickens in the roost following her lead to peck at the chicken. Once her protective feathers are gone, the soft skin is exposed and can be easily punctured by the sharp beaks. When all of the chickens gang up on the one—pecking and puncturing the soft skin—damage, infection, and ultimately death often occurs.

If that makes you cringe or makes you feel sad or disgusted, what we've described is a common occurrence among girls. And it's deeply painful. Bullying, ganging up on others, teasing, and picking on or "pecking" others can result in severe emotional injury and even the death of a girl's self-esteem.

More support to stop bullying:

http://www.pacer.org/bullying/
http://www.stopbullying.gov
http://www.sesamestreet.org/parents/topicsandactivities/topics/bullying

There is no joke, prank, or teasing worth damaging another person's self-worth and self-esteem.

Does this mean that popular girls are bad? No, not at all. It just shows that at times people are willing to do crazy things to be seen as popular or accepted into a group.

The important thing to remember is what may seem popular may not make sense, and that's okay. You don't have to participate. What does make sense is YOU holding true to yourself and not lowering your standards to "fit in".

Kidspeak: "There are different types of popular: Those who are out-going and nice to everyone and then the bullies who are mean and feared by everyone. Everyone loves the nice people. As for the bullies, people are only their friends to make allies with them so they aren't the ones being bullied by them."

Should I try to be, look, and act like everyone at school to fit in?

A great question because it means you're smart enough to realize you can be whomever you want to be. What you might be looking for is permission. Well, here it is: We're giving you permission to be yourself. Be true to your core. Be true to what you know in your heart is right. Be true to your values without compromising them because of what another person says or convinces you to do.

You might ask, "Why shouldn't I change who I am to fit in? I want to be popular." Here's the thing: If you change who you are to be popu-lar, then what will you do when what is popular changes again?

Let's say that you have a green shirt that you just love to wear. It has these cool silver buttons and little stitches on the sleeve that are so unique. You love the way the fabric feels against your skin. But one day someone says, "Green is not the color for us. Let's all wear blue. If you want to fit in, you should ditch the green and wear blue."

You look longingly at your favorite green shirt. It's the best shirt you've ever owned, but you can't wear it if you really want to fit in. So you give the shirt away to a thrift store. Then you sort through your closet and drawers and get rid of all of your green clothes because it's so important that you fit in. The next day at school, you wear your blue shirt even though the tag itch-

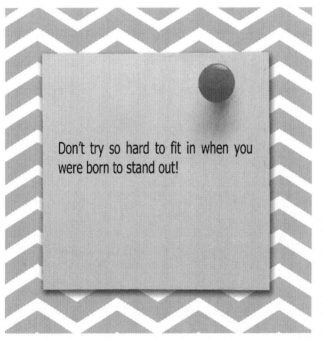

es and you hate the way the left sleeve catches on your backpack.

Two weeks later, that same someone comes to school wearing your favorite green shirt. Everyone loves the shiny buttons. "Hey guys, blue is out! Green is totally in. Don't you love my new shirt?"

"Didn't you have a shirt like that?" the girl sitting next to you asks. "You should wear it tomorrow."

This example is to help you see that styles, clothing, hairstyles, makeup, EVERYTHING is constantly changing! If you're so busy trying to change yourself to fit in with friend A, B, C, or D, you will lose yourself in the process.

Enjoy who you are. Celebrate your unique tastes. If you have a favorite shirt or pair of jeans or a skirt that you love and it looks nice, then wear it. Who cares what the "popular" girl says is in style? You don't have to be a copy of someone else to be liked. It's okay to have your own special flair that shows off your true beauty.

Each one of us has unique features that we should be proud of and love about ourselves. Your hair color, your type of hair (whether it be wavy, straight, curly, thick, or fine), color of your eyes, shape of your body, and tone of your voice. These are what you were born with because it matches who you are. Remember a modest, well-dressed, clean, smiling girl will fit in at any time in any situation!

When in doubt of how to be or act, follow the Golden Rule. In essence, this rule says to treat others the way you would like to be treated.

Often kids and teenagers experience peer pressure—influence from someone who is around the same age as you. Peer pressure doesn't always have to be a negative thing, but that's usually what you'll hear it referred to as. It occurs when an individual or group tries to get you to do something, typically something that you disagree with.

It's hard to believe, but every year, thousands of kids are injured in terrible accidents and some even die as a result of peer pressure. When questioned later, those injured kids say they wish they would have listened to what they knew was right inside.

One of those terrible accidents included five teenagers. Rachelle heard about this accident when she was a teenager. Each of these kids had been taught how important it is to wear seatbelts in a car, but one of the kids said, "Seatbelts are dumb," and didn't wear it. Another decided they didn't want to look "dumb" by wearing a seatbelt so they didn't buckle up either. Only two kids wore their seatbelts and the other three did not. When the car crashed, those three kids were thrown from the car. One went through the windshield and died instantly. Another broke his back and will never walk again. And the third had a broken arm, broken leg, cuts, and bruises. The two kids who wore their seatbelts had bruises and minor injuries, but they were nothing like those of the kids who didn't wear their seatbelts. Families were damaged by grief and these kids were haunted by the choice they had made to be "cool" and "fit in" for the rest of their lives.

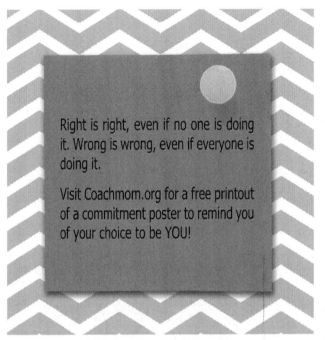

Right is right, even if no one is doing it. Wrong is wrong, even if everyone is doing it.

Visit Coachmom.org for a free printout of a commitment poster to remind you of your choice to be YOU!

Now that you've read this chapter, how about you answer your own question: Should I act like everyone else?

Wearing a seatbelt might be an easy thing to decide, but what will you do when everyone is smoking? Or someone tells you to take a pill to fit in and feel good about yourself? What about if you're at a party and everyone is passing around beer?

The time to decide those things is now. And if you will decide now, you won't have to decide again. There will come a time when you are tested, so make the decision now to be true to yourself. Make the decision that you will always wear your seatbelt, never smoke or take drugs, never drink, and never make poor choices because someone else says that it's cool.

Take the CoachMom challenge to make peer pressure a positive thing in your life by being an example of goodness, happiness, and smart choices. You can be an influence for good on those around you. Take the challenge at coachmom.org.

Kidspeak: "Many of the 'popular' girls were trying to decide what was popular and what was just plain dumb or ugly to wear. Well, by now I was pretty sick and tired of this and decided I was done with them. The next day I wore a football jersey I liked and they tried to talk me out of wearing it, but I liked it and didn't listen. The next few days I was surprised to find almost every girl in the popular group was wearing a football jersey of her own. They told me they were just changing up the style. I had to smile about that."

SUPER SENTENCES

I know _____ is a good friend because she

_____.

I don't need to do wrong to feel right.

One way I feel secure is

_____.

I fight gossip and negative words by

_____.

One thing I can do this week to strengthen a true friendship is to

_____.

My Thoughts...

Chapter 9: School

Scenario: *Kylie didn't get her homework done because she was hanging out with friends. She had to miss Fun Friday at school and stay inside to do math problems. She felt frustrated and then she started to worry about how she would handle all of the classes, homework, and different things coming up in middle school. She wanted to take Honors English but none of her friends were, and now Kylie wasn't sure she could handle it.*

I'm starting middle school/junior high and I'm scared. How do I handle the change?

This is a big change. You're graduating from elementary school and moving up. Most of the time when we feel scared it's because we don't have enough information. Have you ever had to walk through a room in the middle of the night that looks kind of spooky? Then you flip the switch and realize what looked like a person was actually the vacuum with your backpack hanging from the handle?

Let's turn on the light and look at this new experience of middle school/junior high. We're confident that you'll be able to handle the changes, because you're inquisitive and working hard to learn. We know this because you're reading this book!

✓ First, don't be afraid to ask questions. Ask your teacher, ask your parents, and ask someone who is older than you who attends that school.

✓ Second, take a tour of the school and check out some of the classes you'll be taking soon.

✓ Third, practice opening a locker combination and don't stress about this! If you have problems, there is always someone to help.

✓ Fourth, talk to your parents about what might be stressful to you. Create plans to make this transition as smooth as possible.

✓ Fifth, be confident in your ability to learn and grow. Have a great attitude and enjoy this new experience.

Kidspeak: "I was terrified to start junior high. Before school started I decided that I was going to make the best of it and be as happy as I could be. I knew it would be a new beginning and that I would be getting a fresh start because I would be going to a new school with a bunch of kids I didn't know. While this scared me, I was eager to start over knowing that those bullies who picked on me in grade school would no longer be a problem in junior high. I looked forward to having lots of classes in one day, making it so that I wasn't surrounded by the same kids all day. It provided an opportunity for me to make new friends and not be around the same kids all of the time. I think one of the main problems in elementary that led to bullying is that we be-

came too comfortable with each other. I looked forward to the change in junior high."

I'm afraid sixth-grade will be too hard. What if I fail? What about middle-school?

Because you are growing up, you're able to handle more classes. You will only fail if you don't try, so that's not going to happen. You'll have a detailed schedule, and after the first few days of school, everything will seem pretty normal. People adapt quickly to new situations, so you'll learn the rhythm of the school and what you need to do to get to class on time. You'll also learn what's expected of you as far as homework and assignments.

There won't be recess anymore, and sometimes that is a hard adjustment, but you'll enjoy the new structure of middle school. You'll have so many different classes with usually a new teacher for each class, which will keep things active and make the day go by quickly.

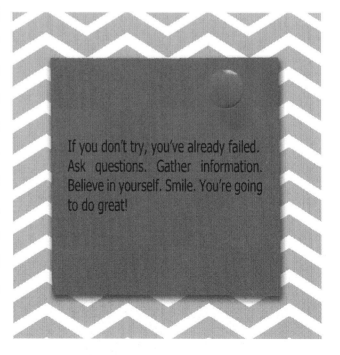

Remember what you've learned so far in this book. Ask questions. Gather information. Believe in yourself. Smile. You're going to do great!

Kidspeak: "Try your hardest! If you do your best, your teachers will know and they won't let you fail. Be involved, participate in class, pay attention, and get your homework in on time. If you run into times where you forget your homework or perform poorly on a test, communicate with your teachers. They want you to succeed as well—it isn't one-sided. They are there to help you, and they will help if they know there is a problem. They teach over a hundred kids a day, so you will need to notify them if you are in need of extra help. Just don't wait until the last week of the term to play catch-up, because it may be too late."

Is it dumb to want to try out for things like honors classes, band, or sports? What if my friends aren't?

It's wonderful to try out for new things. It is so awesome that you are willing to try! This is a time in your life where you get to explore lots of options to learn what you are interested in. Don't hesitate to try new things. You'll never know if you like something if you don't give it a shot.

What if your friends don't want to try anything new? That's okay. They are still your friends, and it's okay to want to do different things. Be respectful of and kind about differences in opinion. At the same time, be encouraging. Maybe your friends need a little hope and support from you to try something new.

If you try out for something and don't make it, you haven't failed. It just means that right now at this time in your life, you are taking a slightly different path. If it's something that is super important to you, then take the time to ask questions and learn what you need to do to improve so that you can make the team or class in the future.

Kidspeak: "If you want to do something you like then do it. It is a new opportunity to make friends and can help you to succeed and adjust to the changes in a new school more than anything else can. Try out for as many new things as you can. It is fun and will help to build your self-esteem!"

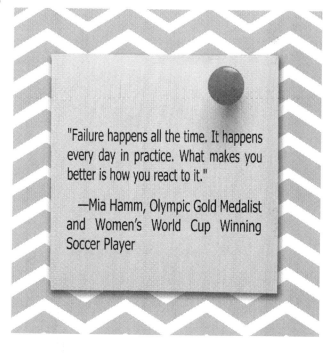

"Failure happens all the time. It happens every day in practice. What makes you better is how you react to it."

—Mia Hamm, Olympic Gold Medalist and Women's World Cup Winning Soccer Player

SUPER SENTENCES

I can do difficult things!

One tough experience or goal in my life that I did great in was

_____.

One way I can face a new situation with confidence is by

_____.

I can manage my time by

_____.

I can try new things, no matter the outcome. One thing I want to try is

_____.

My Thoughts...

Chapter 10: Dreams & Goals

Scenario: *When the author Rachelle was in sixth grade she took a career test. She said she wanted to be an author. When she got the results back, it said that an author wasn't a good occupation because there wasn't a steady income. She was advised to choose a new occupation. Rachelle felt sad about this because she loved writing, but she looked into other options. In the end, she decided to keep writing and work on her goal. At the publication of this book, Rachelle has written hundreds of poems and over a dozen books.*

I think I know what I want to be when I grow up, but can I change my mind later?

Great job thinking about your bright future! There are so many possibilities. Right now, nothing is set in stone. You have many years ahead to explore the different paths of education, jobs, and ways to contribute. Don't be afraid to study a variety of ideas or interests and find out what is required for each one. Talk to people about their work. Ask them how they became an accountant, a piano teacher, a sculptor, a hairdresser, an engineer, etc. Research the internet on approved sites for what you like and can see yourself doing.

When you have a clearer picture of a few interests, create a plan. This could be three simple goals to achieve in life, three goals for the year, or simply a paragraph that tells what you want to do in three, five, or even ten years from now.

To be more specific, use the "Create a Mini Life Plan" ideas found in the Just for Mom section (Chapter 10). Together with your mom or individually, you can follow the simple three-step instructions.

If you want to simply brainstorm right now, begin with three to five (or more!) things you want to do, learn, or accomplish over the coming year. Look at skills needed. Remember to include the fun, fabulous, and adventurous to make it a whole package.

Next, write down three to five things that you want to accomplish and experience three years from now. Lastly, write down three to five dreams and goals for five years from now. This is also a great activity to do with your parents and family. They can share ideas or suggestions on making dreams come true. Share what you feel comfortable with and ask for their advice in making these dreams a reality.

Your life is before you. Think about what you want it to look, feel, and be like. Then plan small, simple, and enjoyable goals to start on that path. Each goal, effort, and thought draws you closer to making these dreams and goals a reality.

Kidspeak: "Just like you did when you were a little kid, you change what you want to be every week, and you can still change your mind now. Even now as we are learning new subjects in school and finding things that we are interested in, our career paths may change. In junior high, you have counselors who meet with you each year to discuss what fields you are interested in and help you plan your classes accordingly to help you prepare for college. They know your goals and interests will change; that is why they meet with us yearly. It is normal."

I want to do great things, but I'm not very good at setting goals. What if I can't achieve them? What if people think my dreams and goals are dumb?

Many people struggle to set and achieve goals. One reason is that it can feel overwhelming at first. There is a saying that applies here: "How do you eat an elephant? One bite at a time." It sounds weird, but it simply means you must break down goals into "chewable" chunks.

Another way to explain it is to reference an incredible swimming athlete, Michael Phelps. Have you ever heard of him? He is one of the greatest Olympians in history. Michael Phelps won an unprecedented *eight gold medals* in swimming at the Summer Olympics in Beijing, China, in 2008. This guy must be part fish. Michael was only 23 years old when he smashed seven world records in one week. Despite the fact that he won eight gold medals in Beijing, he is also the highest achieving Olympian of all time, with a total of 18 gold medals in the 118-year history of the modern Olympics. http://en.wikipedia.org/wiki/Michael_Phelps

Michael was asked how he could focus so clearly when he had 17 total races, eight of which were finals. He said, "By taking it one step at a time. One race at a time, and once they were finished, move on."

This is exactly what we must do with our own goals: break big goals into smaller, more manageable goals. It's a pretty simple process if you follow the gold medalists and do something like this:

- ✓ Believe in yourself
- ✓ Set goals
- ✓ Believe in yourself
- ✓ Break big goals into smaller, manageable steps
- ✓ Believe in yourself
- ✓ Work hard and achieve those goals!

Let's put these ideas into real life. Say that your goal is to become a teacher, an artist, or a doctor and travel through Europe (England, Germany, France, etc.). I'm going to show you how those goals can be broken down into bite-size pieces. You might be surprised to see that the beginning steps are similar for each goal.

My Dream: Become a teacher, artist, or doctor and travel through Europe

My Goals:

- ✓ Get good grades (As and Bs) through high school; graduate with a GPA of 3.75 or more
- ✓ Interview three teachers, artists, or doctors to learn more about what, how, and how much they do.
- ✓ Research three universities and their programs.
- ✓ Volunteer to help in the job I've chosen. Do a "shadow day" to watch them work or help afterschool/in the summer at their workplace.

✓ Apply for scholarships and enroll in the college of my choice. Keep making goals and breaking them down into "bites."

✓ Go on a study abroad program through the college or another program to Europe.

✓ Graduate from college with a degree.

✓ Make a difference in the community, state, and world with one thing I can do in my job.

Try using our Super Sentence cards as you achieve one small goal during this coming week. It could be something like going to bed on time every night, practicing your musical instrument for an allotted time, exercising three times this week, or even doing five acts of service. At the end of the week, think about how it went: what worked, what didn't work, what do you want to do differently? Make one change to better your efforts.

Setting goals is the difference between successful people and those who are still dreaming. Don't be afraid to reach for the stars. You can do amazing things!
—Coach Mom

In a few short weeks, you can change behaviors, implement great plans, and improve yourself in surprising ways.

Lastly, a word about discouragement. Everyone feels frustrated when trying to achieve a goal. It's not a quick fix. Each effort, sacrifice, and choice for achieving adds up and makes a difference. When you feel discouraged try these tips:

✓ Talk with your mom. Share your feelings and get them out. That usually helps.

✓ Read your journal or items in your treasure box. Remember the happiness you felt in achieving one goal or when one good thing happened in trying.

✓ Listen to uplifting music that makes you feel like "Oh yeah, I GOT THIS!"

✓ Do one thing to move a goal forward, even if it's teeny-tiny.

✓ Take a nap—sometimes we're overwhelmed and simply need to rest.

✓ Read motivational stories or books of kids or even adults who have done great things. Great sites to visit with your mom include: http://kidsareheroes.org/, http://listverse.com/2011/01/27/10-great-philanthropists-who-are-kids/, and http://www.cbsnews.com/news/60-minutes-presents-amazing-kids/.

Kidspeak: "Get help with setting goals. Always start with small goals, keeping your end goal in mind and working up to it. If you have to, write reminders down or set timers to help you remember to do something. Don't let distractions keep you from accomplishing your goals. Don't worry about what others think about your dreams; their dreams are different. If it is your dream to do something, then do it. Don't base your dreams and goals off of what someone else says. It is your opinion that matters most when trying to reach what you want."

Super Sentences

I can succeed because I know how to

_____.

My dream is to _____.

One goal that will help achieve my dream is

_____.

My mom can help me realize my dream by

_____.

I can do better at goal-achieving by

_____.

[Download a fun Weekly Goal sheet to post at www.coachmom.org or www.conniesokol.com]

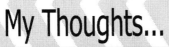

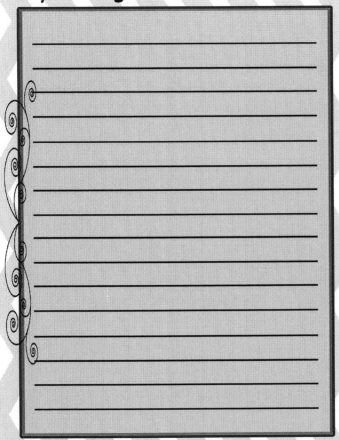

Just for Moms

Just for Moms

A famous quote states, "There is no way to be a perfect mother and a million ways to be a good one."[1] Thank goodness! We can let that expectation go and start enjoying being a mother again.

In our unique situations, we tend to go through similar stages, experiences, and issues. Years ago women met and talked at the washing well, sharing all the good, bad, and the ugly, and headed home happier for it. We no longer have the physical washing well, but we still have each other. That means we can share thoughts, ideas, and suggestions for how to not only survive raising our daughters but thrive in doing it.

The following sections give specific tips and insights just for you, the mom. They are not the last word. They are for reading, considering, and applying in a way that works best for you. For more questions or connection with other moms, go to www.coachmom.org or www.conniesokol.com for the hub of what's happening in motherhood.

Meanwhile, enjoy these next few pages for what they are—a collection of motherly wisdom, love, and support just for you!

Best,

Rachelle and Connie

Chapter 11: Why You're a Fabulous Mother and How to Stay Fabulous!

That's right. You're fabulous because you are choosing to become the best mother you can be. And because you want to help your daughter become her best self, too.

You're also fabulous because...

- ✓ you picked up this book with a desire to further connect with your daughter.
- ✓ you realize there are lots of questions your daughter may have but may or may not ask.
- ✓ you're seeking for an opportunity to let her open up and ask.
- ✓ you want to better understand your daughter, what her needs are, and how to meet those needs.

Because of your desires, those opportunities and moments to connect will come. When they do come, you will be prepared. That's because of your life experience, your love for your daughter, and reading this book.

Ways to Stay Fabulous

At times we mothers can be hard on ourselves, especially in relation to how we parent: Are we doing okay? Are our children thriving? Are we missing the mark? When it's one of those days and you're feeling very non-fabulous, read through or try one of these can-dos.

1. **Recognize the good you're doing.** Ignore uninvited negative responses from children or others (quips, eye-rolling, critical remarks, etc.). Don't judge yourself by the outcome of your children. Focus on your energy, efforts, and what you can appropriately control.

2. **Regularly verbally and physically reward your efforts.** Positive self-talk, meaningful rewards during the week or at the end, "time out" for good behavior, and other rewards can keep you going. Verbalize daily appreciation phrases such as, "I did well today by..." or "Kudos to me for...." (e.g. not beating the dog). Things like that. These are best done in front of the mirror (embarrassing but powerful).

3. **Connect with other women.** Get ideas, ask questions, find resources, and check out viable sites like www.coachmom.org or www.conniesokol.com. As you chat with other women you'll find helpful allies and insightful solutions. Check out hobby groups, church connections, community causes, school commitments, and more. This connection to others is vital. Start small and keep at it. Before you know it you'll have a "team" supporting you in motherhood.

4. **Set realistic expectations of yourself.** Do not compare yourself with others. Simply do not. No matter the "expected" growth timeline for your motherhood stage, adjust for your situation, family, and emotional well-being. As we are healthy in *our* expectations, it will positively affect our children, making them and us happier. In their development and in your personal joy, choose to focus on a few key areas during a season of life. Then move forward knowing that whatever areas remain will take their proper place or be dealt with later.

Connie shares: As the mother of a child with Asperger's Syndrome, I've had many moments of adjusting my expectations. I remember taking my son to a "joyful music" experience. The other elementary-aged children played the musical instruments as instructed and moved to the music in appropriate lunges and choreographed turns. My son spent his time loudly playing under the grand piano and running in circles. I spent my time chasing him. Finally, it hit me—he wasn't like other kids and therefore needed a different "joyful" experience. I scooped him up with my other children and took them to the park. Fresh air, plenty of run-around space, and no dirty looks. Perfect.

5. **Remember the honor, privilege, and divine wonder of being a mother.** It's easy to forget, but when we remember our purpose, we find the meaning in our daily dos. A few years ago I received the surprise gift of having a seventh child, a baby caboose at the age of 46! During that same time—unexpectedly, my first trimester—I had also contracted with a publisher to write a book on motherhood. Lovely. I would describe the wonders of motherhood while being sick as a dog. However, surprisingly that experience became a lodestar in my percep-

tion on motherhood. Each day I spent beautiful hours researching the incredible reality and divinity of motherhood. Not only did I write *Motherhood Matters* in one of the shortest timeframes I'd experienced, but my love and admiration for the role of motherhood magnified and deepened in a life-changing way.

6. Keep your I'm-a-fabulous-mother bucket filled. We need to recognize when the bucket gets empty, what depletes it, and what fills it.

Here's one suggestion: Consider jotting thoughts in a "Good Job" journal in response to these thoughtful questions. Do one or a few or all!

What do you feel you've done well so far in parenting (listening, being organized, being fun, etc.)?

What is one experience you remember when you felt you had succeeded with a child?

What is one challenge you've overcome in parenting?

What is one aspect of motherhood that was a struggle? What is one thing you did to make it a positive?

What is one piece of advice from someone else that has worked for you?

What is one thing you'd like to do differently right now in your parenting?

Besides receiving love, appreciation, and respect from your family, what are some ways you would love to be rewarded for what you do as a mother? (Include tangible and nontangible rewards, e.g. pedicure, love notes, hugs, verbal praise, etc.)

What is one way you can reward yourself TODAY for all you've done as a mother?

Motherhood, in all its wonder, can at times be a lonely business with few compliments and great expectations. Take a moment to consider what you're already doing well. Feel free to share at www.coachmom.org and www.conniesokol.com. Find out what other moms are saying, read uplifting and informational blog posts, and find support and connection with other mothers.

Chapter 12: Keys to Connected Conversations

You've read the kid questions, maybe even the kids' section (good thinking), and now you are ready to roll on the conversation. Just one more thing. Consider what you want that conversation to look like. More important than a one-time boost of let's-chat energy, you can create a pattern of healthy, enjoyable, natural conversations for long-term benefits.

As relationship author Dr. John Gottman shares, how a conversation starts indicates to a 97% degree how it will end. To successfully get the ball rolling use Connection First, Convo Jumpstarts, and Icebreaker Ideas.

** CONNECTION FIRST **

Before you Begin

1. Don't beat around the bush. Kids can smell a hidden agenda. It's good to be up front with your daughter about what you want to do.

Try something like, "Hey, I saw this cute book and thought of you. It's got a bunch of great questions that kids have asked who are in 6th grade, secrets they want to know about. So fun. I'd love to choose a couple and chat for a few minutes, get your opinion, what you think. Do you want to try it tonight or this weekend?"

2. Start with something comfortable. Casual, non-threatening, broad questions such as, "How was school," "How was the sport/afterschool activity," etc. open the gate in a simple way. Information or fact type of conversation starters create safe ground. Your child doesn't have to risk much. And they get to choose how deep they want to go. This gives them a healthy feeling of control in a conversation.

3. Move to more specific. Funnel your questions to ones with more relationship or feeling words (e.g. "How is Susie doing with her sprained ankle?" "Who did you hang out with at recess today?" "Is Kelly being more kind today?") See how much your child opens up and how ready they are for talking. Follow her lead, after giving a little nudge.

Make the Moment Successful

1. **Find a good time for both of you.** This could be Sunday, an evening, or even driving home from an activity—whatever feels most natural to both of you.

2. **Keep it short.** About 15 minutes is a baseline—more if she is happy to chat, less if it's way too awkward at first!

3. **Choose one to three questions that most resonate.** You can each take turns choosing or simply choose one for the whole conversation. Then LISTEN to your daughter. Authors Gary and Joy Lundberg of *I Don't Have to Make Everything All Better* recommend to listen, listen, listen and understand.[2] This is key. You're the subtle guide to the conversation, not the overbearing expert. Ask more "find out" questions. Don't preach or share all you know. Use this as a time to observe and feel what your daughter thinks and feels too.

4. **Look for the breadcrumbs.** Your daughter may verbally wander down paths, but as you listen for them, you can pick up on clues such as:

What subject do they keep coming back to (boys, friendship issues, weight, etc.)?

What do they light up about/talk easily about?

What seems to be a hot button, something she avoids, or something she seems hesitant to talk about? (Note those for later and carefully address them in later conversations.)

Remember, you want the real deal so don't worry if it doesn't go perfectly. It's about the attempt!

5. **Don't expect perfection.** Some chats will go fabulously, some will feel like a root canal. That's okay, it's a process—it will get better.

6. Include some kind of refreshment. Whether it's ice cream, popcorn, hamburgers, or protein shakes, bring it on. Choose something you both love and forget about the calories just for now. No doubt about it, fun food makes for memorable moments.

7. Finish with a hug, a thank you, and/or a way to let her know you value her thoughts. Even if her viewpoints contradict your own, simply listen and validate. That doesn't mean you agree, just that you're listening. Some good responses are, "Really? I hadn't thought of that," "I could see how you could feel that way," or "What did you think/do/feel next?" For more ideas on how to listen or respond, consider the book *How to Talk So Kids Will Listen & Listen So Kids Will Talk* by Adele Faber and Elaine Mazlish.

Location, Location, Location

Make the location as natural to the conversation as possible. If it requires more privacy, don't hesitate to create it. If you can choose a regular time and spot, all the better. Otherwise, take the moment when it comes.

At the park. Find a quiet tree in a semi-busy park where you can lounge, preferably with a treat (see above!). With people and activity present, but not center stage, you can remove possible pressure on your child to talk.

On a drive home. Not going to an activity, where one or both of you will be preoccupied with what's to come, but a natural post-activity drive could be nicely done. Have three or four questions in mind, or even use our **Convo Card** that contains the 10 Questions in this book as well as Keys to Connection tips.

In her or your room. Close the door so other family members don't interrupt. Keep the lighting low so it doesn't feel like an interrogation. And keep it cozy—sit on the bed in PJs with pillows. Laugh often. Ask her to let you know when your brows furrow or you're getting "Mom-ish."

At a favorite treat place. Oh yes, the familiar refrain of chat and chow. But it works! Maybe it's a favorite shake place, Mexican restaurant, or chic spot. Sometimes kids feel more able to engage in private conversations in a public place—the spotlight is off of them. Choose a more private booth or table, however, and keep your voice to a low minimum (without reverting to Mom serious…).

Doing a shared activity. Maybe she likes jogging, tennis, hiking, painting, designing, movie-watching, etc. Choosing one together is even better. If you can, share the activity and chat while you engage or split it up—do the activity first, then chat, or vice-versa. Use this to loosen up and get in a convo groove before more serious discussion starts.

When You Run into Problems

Consider these common concerns on how to deal with conversation hiccups.

"She won't talk!" Do not force more from her. It may be that she is naturally shy or nonverbal or doesn't necessarily feel emotionally safe talking about these things. That's okay! *Do not take it personally.* Ask yourself if you're doing what you can to make the experience comfortable (e.g. listening; talking in a natural, soothing tone; showing sincere interest in her thoughts and feelings; not talking the entire time; etc.). Then take the success in smaller steps—one question or for a few minutes the first time, a few questions or for five minutes the next time. No matter how it goes, express sincere appreciation for her talking with you and your happiness in doing it.

"I'm afraid I don't know the answers or how to respond." Welcome to the club! As mothers, we're literally all in this together. What matters most to your daughter is that you try. When you come to a place or a question she has and you're unsure, stall with another question such as "Can you tell me a little more what you're thinking or what you mean by that?" or "That's a good question—can you help me understand a little more what you're thinking?" That gives you time to think of a response!

And remember, *less is more.* Sometimes they want a teaspoon and we give them the whole teacup. Keep asking more find-out questions to truly get to the root of what they're needing to know.

"I'm not sure I'm giving her the best answers." The best answer is an honest from-the-heart answer. Perhaps you've made some different choices in your childhood, ones you may not want her to know about. Or maybe you don't really know what is the best way to handle a particular situation. When in doubt, go with your gut. And be honest in your indecision, e.g. "That is a great question; I'm just not sure how to answer that—can I take some time and get back to you?" *Then get back to her.* Otherwise, use the tips, resources, and information we've presented here as a solid springboard. These are time-tested principles and practices that give you a high chance at a positive result.

"We never seem to go deep enough—she just gives a simple yes or no response." Perhaps to start, that's all she's comfortable with and that's okay. Keep trying, perhaps once a week at a standing "Mom and Me" time or once every few weeks with different questions. That said, consider how you're asking the questions. Leave them open-ended. Instead of, "Do you think..." ask questions like "What do you think about..." or "How would you feel if..." and "What would be a helpful thing to do if..."

*** CONVO JUMPSTARTS ***

Getting a conversation going can be joyful or tricky, depending on the child and the subject. Some of the kid questions can feel tender or slightly embarrassing to both them and you. Instead of jumping right into the question, perhaps try some of these starters. (Note: In the "By

Chapter" section of Chapter 13, you can find Starter Qs that are specific to the question).

1. "I love talking with you. Just know that in these chats you can tell me anything—anything you think or feel or want to say. I love hearing your opinions! Speaking of, did you get a chance to flip through the book at all? What did you think so far?"

2. "You know, I was skimming through these questions, and I thought they were great! I seriously wish I had the answers when I was in sixth grade. Some things haven't changed—shocking, I know. Like this one question... (share one). Did you find anything that stuck out to you?"

3. "I'm guessing you already know the answers to some of these questions, just from our chats already. But a few I wasn't so sure about. Were there any questions that piqued your curiosity or interest?"

4. "Okay, I get that some of these could be a little embarrassing. We can do those *later*, much later if you want! Just let me know when you want to chat about them and we can. I'm not stressed about it, so don't worry about that. I'm open to talk about whatever, whenever you want. Okay, you get to choose the first question—what sounded good?"

5. "My friend told me about this book, and I love the cute cover. It has some great questions. Can we take a couple of minutes and try one or

two—we can take turns choosing a question." Wait for her response and then reply, "Super, who do you want to start?"

6. "Hey, did you get a chance to check out that book? I found a question I wish I'd known the answer to when I was twelve. Do you want to give it a shot together?"

7. "You know, I've heard you mention/you shared last week/when we talked the other day about..., and it made me think of this book. It has a lot of great questions that are from kids and answered by kids. Can we take a few minutes? I just wanted to talk about this one. And then if you want to check it out or talk about the others, I'd love to."

Give one or more of these conversation starters a try. If your child is hesitant or still doesn't feel confident in moving the conversation, continue to encourage by example. Say, "No worries, I can go first," and then choose a very non-threatening question.

*** ICEBREAKER IDEAS ***

If your daughter is more of a fun-and-games girl, try something more hands-on. For example, use the My Faves questionnaire below for a casual non-serious way to open the gate. More ideas and games are available at www.coachmom.org or www.conniesokol.com.

MY FAVES!

There are two ways to use the questionnaire:

One, each of you completes the questions with your own answers, then shares with the other. Choose a new topic each time it's your turn or go in order and both share your answers. OR

Two, complete the answer by guessing what the OTHER person's favorite is. Afterward, compare answers and see how close you got.

MY FAVES:

Favorite snack:

_____

Favorite family vacation:

_____

Favorite pet:

_____

Favorite fun time with Mom:

_____

Favorite movie:

_____

Favorite special treasures:

_____

Favorite book:

_____

Favorite sport:

_____

Favorite dinner:

_____

Favorite thing on a Saturday:

_____

Favorite season:

_____

As you've read these connecting conversation ideas, hopefully one or two have resonated and you're excited to try them. Choose one and give it a try!

Chapter 13: Starter Qs, Scenarios, & Super Sentences

In each chapter we share tips just for you, the mom. Feel free to use any of the Starter Qs to get the conversation going. Discuss a scenario (or even two or more) to help your child learn new ways to respond and practice using them in a safe way. Lastly, fill in the Super Sentences individually (she doesn't have to share out loud) or together. You can download fabulous Super Sentence cards from our website to complete and then post on a fun board or wall at www.coachmom.org or www.conniesokol.com.

A WORD ON USING SCENARIOS

Using scenarios are ideal to help your child better understand a situation. It also is an excellent way to prepare her for a real-time issue. She can anticipate the problem and know clear solutions, having already role-played a similar experience.

Let's take one scenario and go through it in detail. You don't need to be as in-depth when discussing scenarios from the mom's "By Chapter" sections (one scenario is also found in each chapter of the girls' section). Do what you feel best. But this will give you an idea of a few possibilities.

SCENARIO

Marissa and Jane are talking at recess. You walk up to the group to say hi. They are talking about how much they weigh. After telling each other how much they weigh, they ask you about your weight. What do you do?

Feelings First:

You're likely feeling awkward and put on the spot. Coming to the group, you weren't thinking you would be sharing this kind of information. And it feels a little competitive, like they're trying to be the lowest number there. But you're confused why this matters, and maybe a bit afraid that your number is higher than everyone else's.

Remember, then respond:

Meaning, *remember what you know to be right for you.* Weight is a personal issue. You don't have to tell anyone this information and likely shouldn't. The other girls would be wise to keep that a private matter too. Each girl's body is a different shape and changes at a different rate, depending on their hormones, when puberty starts, genetics (what kind of body type they inherited through birth), and many other factors. To compare is the beginning of unhappiness. Stop the comparison and you will help both yourself and your friends have healthier conversations and stronger friendships.

Choose your Words:

In this situation, here are a few possible ways to respond:

- "Actually, I keep that private. It helps me stay focused on being healthy, not trying to be super skinny. By the way, do you guys know when we're supposed to turn in (x) assignment?" [Try to go back to your original reason for joining the group, having the conversation, or doing the activity.]

- "You know what's funny is that I don't think weight [or how big a certain body part is, etc.] matters. What matters to me is the good friends you guys are. I love that we can be ourselves and talk about things that are fun or important. Do you want to go [do another activity]?"

- "Oh, I don't worry about that. I like my weight. But it *is* funny to me what my body does sometimes. Have you guys noticed...?" [Share something else that is a real concern, like getting taller or hair in your armpits!]

Each scenario shares a different way to respond. That depends on how you feel and what's a more natural way to talk. In the last scenario you talk about body issues, which you likely want to talk about anyway. But it does it in an exploring way rather than a competitive way. It's not about who has the "right" body or weight or shape, it's about what have each of you noticed and learning from it.

This is called **exploratory conversation,** because you explore rather than assign what's best. These are good kinds of conversations to have. Everyone is allowed their opinion and experience. No one has to be right or "win."

Terms

Exploratory conversation: everyone shares their opinion and experience; no one is best or "wins."

Scenario: a pretend situation to practice your response before the real one happens.

Opinion: your thoughts or feelings on a subject.

Convo Clue Finders:

Did you find the key words to remember and use in the future? Here are some of them:

"Actually" This creates a feeling of being an authority on yourself. You know how you feel.

"I" These kinds of "I" statements take responsibility for your own thoughts and actions. They don't point a finger. They simply state how you feel and what you can or can't do.

"By the way" A change-up phrase (a phrase that changes direction of a conversation or action), this helps you take the focus off the current question or conversation. If you feel what's being talked about or done is not right or good, try first to distract or change the conversation. Other change-up phrases can be "Do you want to [do another activity]?" or "Not to interrupt, but do you guys want to…"

"What matters to me" A feeling phrase, this helps you own what you want to do and share it in a kind way. Some other feeling phrases are "I would rather…" or "My vote would be to…"

"Have you noticed" These are opinion phrases. You offer someone else the chance to share their opinion or thoughts. It doesn't mean you agree with them; you're just listening to what they think. Other opinion phrases could be "What do you think?" or "What do you want to do?"

Quick Phrases

"I" statements: I feel... I would like to... I'm frustrated that...

Change-up phrases: Do you want to... I'd rather talk about... How about we do (x) right now...

Feeling phrases: I would rather... My vote would be to...

Opinion phrases: What do you think? What do you want to do?

Chapter 14: By Chapter: Girls' Questions in Detail

In this section, we'll share more information, conversation suggestions, and mom support on each of the 10 Girls' Questions.

Chapter 1: Beauty & Body Image

How do I know if I'm pretty?

Some girls are developing faster than I am. Is there something wrong with me?

What about my skin—do I need to wear makeup? What do I do with a zit?

As a mother, you well know the barrage of negative body and beauty messages our children receive on a daily basis. The most common message: You're not pretty without makeup. One study showed that over half of twelve- to fourteen-year-olds wear makeup most of the time, with about 17% *refusing to leave the house* without makeup on.[3] Where do these messages come from and how do we combat them?

The answer: Doing what you're doing—reading this book. Small things can make a big difference if we are intentional. Become aware of repeated themes in your daughter's comments and conversations. Notice her actions—is she spending more time in front of the mirror? Does she complain about her skin or how she looks? Does she worry about being attractive to boys? At this age, it's natural for your once-tomboy to take a sudden interest in doing her hair and wearing nice clothes. And, it's a great time for this chapter's conversation on what makes someone truly beautiful.

Beauty inside and out. Ask your daughter one or two of the Starter Qs—who do you think is beautiful? What do you think makes someone beautiful? Emphasize the importance of beauty being an inside-out deal. Real beauty is something we want to look at, feel, or enjoy being around. It's related to how you feel with someone. A wrinkled grandma looks and feels beautiful to a child because the grandma cares about and loves her, does good things for, and serves her. When you discover who your child feels happiest and most self-confident around, you can help her discover true keys to real beauty.

Applying make-up at a young age not only blocks pores and increases chances for bacteria (which worsens the cycle of make-up use) but can have long-term effects on skin such as drying and irritability.

A Kaiser Foundation study shows that in movies, TV shows, and accompanying commercials, more than half the female characters had comments made about their looks, compared to 24% of male characters.

Developing at different rates. For more specific information on body changes, read Chapter 5 on Puberty. That will give you answers to possible questions. But first, assure her that each person's body changes at a different rate, according to how her body chemistry is designed.

In the developmental timeline, there is not a right or wrong, better or worse, good or bad. What is important is that she feels healthy and strong. Let her know that worrying about how big her chest is (or isn't) is normal but not necessary. Some girls get hips and a chest quick, some stay lean and lanky throughout high school. Help her understand that each body type is beautiful and necessary to create diversity and beauty as a whole.

We all have different body types. In her book, *Faithful, Fit & Fabulous*, Connie references studies by psychologist William Sheldon and physician Jean Vague[4] on six body types:

Ectomorphs—high metabolism, naturally thin

Mesomorphs—strong and fit, moderate metabolism, natural muscle
tone

Endomorphs—large-boned, full-bodied, slower metabolism

Add to the above the researchers' enhancements of "pear" or "apple" shapes:

Pear—generally curvy with smaller waists, rounder backsides, and
fuller hips/thighs

Apple—usually slender with long, lean legs and weight residing in
stomach area

Combining the two gives you a general idea of your body type. Why is that important? Because understanding how your body is *designed* to look gives you personal power. You appreciate your shape, accept it's not likely to fundamentally change, and embrace its unique strengths.

Use these tips to discuss more Starter Qs below on ways to feel and be more beautiful, inside and out.

Just for Mom Tips

Smile. This small act has a power-packed result. A study in the *European Journal of Social Psychology* shared that smiling makes you more attractive and approachable. This will matter most to your daughter! And smiling lowers stress and anxiety, releases endorphins (a feel-good hormone), and makes you feel comfortable in awkward situations.[5]

Be kind. Simply serving others or speaking kindly makes a difference in how you feel about and see yourself and how others see you. A UC Berkley study showed that when people are kind, give of themselves and their time, and show caring attitudes toward others, they receive all kinds of benefits. Notably, more positive hormones release to create a "warm glow" effect—in essence, making you appear more beautiful, feel more gratitude, and make more social connections.[6]

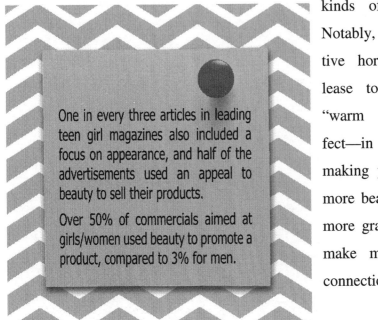

One in every three articles in leading teen girl magazines also included a focus on appearance, and half of the advertisements used an appeal to beauty to sell their products.

Over 50% of commercials aimed at girls/women used beauty to promote a product, compared to 3% for men.

Establish self-identity. When your daughter knows who she truly is—a person of value and worth simply because she exists—accepting her personal beauty will be easier. In both authors' views, we believe ourselves to be children of God. And as such, we come from a divine heritage. We can teach our children that who we are is lasting and purposeful; that inside we are strong, lovely, and wonderful; and that we each have something unique to contribute to this world and others. A healthy self-identity leads to more joy and less comparing.

STARTER Qs

➤ Who do you think is beautiful? What do you think makes someone beautiful?

➤ At the times you feel good about yourself, what are you doing? Who are you with?

➤ What is one body part you have inherited? Who in your family also has that? How have they responded positively?

➤ We all have different body types. Have you noticed that? How can you appreciate *your* body more fully?

➤ Our bodies change at different times—how can you avoid comparing to someone else?

SCENARIOS

> You're standing in a group at school when one of the girls points out you have a zit, a birthmark, or something wrong with your face or body. How do you respond?

> At lunch someone tells what bra size they're wearing. All the girls start comparing sizes. What do you do?

> Your friends read some glam magazines for fun. After a while you don't feel so good about yourself. Why do you think that is? What can you say or do?

SUPER SENTENCES

I appreciate my _____(body part) because

_____!

I feel beautiful when _____.

I know I'm beautiful because _____.

Beauty, inside and out, to me means

_____.

One thing I can do to feel and become more beautiful, inside and out, is

_____

_____.

In a study on elementary-aged children, both boys and girls told researchers they were dissatisfied with their bodies after watching a music video with Britney Spears and a TV segment of *Friends.*

"Fast Facts," Teen Health and the Media—Body Image and Nutrition, https://depts.washington.edu/thmedia/view.cgi?section=bodyimage&page=fastfacts

Chapter 2: Weight Worries

Should I be worried about my weight?

Should I go on diets with my friends?

How do I know if my mom is being nice or being honest about my weight?

Whether it's appropriate or not, sixth-grade girls are worried about weight. A survey by the National Heart, Lung, and Blood Institute found that girls as young as nine and ten years old have already tried to *lose weight.*[7]

As a mother, reassure your daughter that weight is not something to worry about—health is. Turn her focus toward feeling fit, strong, and healthy. Show her an example of good eating habits (imperfect as we may be) and positive attempts to stay active in daily life. Direct her attention away from numbers on a scale—no matter if they are a valid concern or not. This will yield immediate and lifelong benefits.

If your daughter's weight is a valid concern, thoughtfully approach it. Be crea-

A 1996 study found an association between the amount of time a child watches movies and music videos with his/her desire to be thin.

One study reported that by age thirteen, 53% of American girls are "unhappy with their bodies." By the time they hit seventeen, the number grows to 78%.

"Fast Facts," Teen Health and the Media—Body Image and Nutrition, https://depts.washington.edu/thmedia/view.cgi?section=bodyimage&page=fastfacts

tive. One woman shared this experience: "In sixth grade my mother helped me lose some 'baby fat' without me realizing it. She told me she wanted to be healthier and asked if I would wake up each morning with her and walk to the hospital. I loved spending time with her. I never knew it was to help me lose a little baby fat—I found that out years later. I wrote about what my mom did in a college paper on children and weight. My professor said it was the most positive way she had ever heard of to help a child who was having weight issues." Find a way that positively connects both you and your daughter and you'll find more lasting success with the weight concern.

Lastly, when speaking about these issues, remember to use tactful but truthful words. She will be sensitive to any lies or half-truths. Always begin with her self-worth—that she is a person, not a number. Make sure she knows that a healthy body weight is one part of who she is, not all of her. Redirect her focus to the positive actions and thoughts she can create in daily life rather than bemoan difficult body issues she may be facing.

If she asks, "Am I fat?" be kind and gentle. Ask her that question back: "What matters most is what you think and feel—do you think you are? Why do you think that?" If she has weight issues, help her learn about healthy behaviors and beliefs without forcing them on her. If she has no weight issues but a negative mental perception, continue to identify unhealthy perceptions (but in a kind way) and help her emphasize the positives in herself and her life.

Actively use the Super Sentences to rewire those negative neural pathways (deep brain grooves of belief that develop habits). Create a new perception that you can support and strengthen.

STARTERS Qs

- ➤ You know, this is a question that might come up… have you ever been asked by friends how much you weigh? Why do you think others worry about weight at your age?
- ➤ What do you think about someone asking you that question?
- ➤ Have you ever thought about how much you weigh? When was the first time you thought about it?
- ➤ What do you think about dieting? Do you know much about how it affects your body?
- ➤ What do you think are some healthy eating behaviors? What about healthy activities? Which would you like to try?
- ➤ Do you think at age twelve you should be thinking about weight? What do you think you should be thinking about at your age? What are your interests, hobbies, daily life dos?

SUPER SENTENCES

Being me is GREAT because

_____.

I love _____ about myself.

My top three talents are: _____, _____,

and _____.

New talents I want to develop are

_____.

I love my body because it can _____.

One thing I can do to be a healthier and happier me is

_____.

Chapter 3: Being Me!

Do I need permission to be myself?

Should I be afraid to be who I am?

Can I make a difference?

The years between six and fourteen are a developmental whirl-wind. Your daughter is becoming more self-aware, independent, and individual, discerning who she is and who she wants to become. In short, she is establishing her self-identity.

As mothers, we help this development by instilling confidence, offering support, and giving guidance. We can be better attuned to their needs and understand their emotional shifts.

Consider a few of these simple suggestions:

Have frequent connecting conversations. Definitely like the one you're about to have on this topic. But also in everyday life and situations. For example, my daughter and I were driving to a school activity, and in the natural flow of conversation some friendship issues arose. By asking a few key, thoughtful questions, I understood the root of the problem, what had been done to resolve it, and my daughter's feelings about the whole situation. She felt heard and I felt relieved! Look for those moments in the simplicity of routine—doing carpool, stopping for a quick ice cream, sitting on her bed and chatting about to-dos. Awareness of those opportunities leads to utilizing them. A chat or a comment can help your daughter's confidence and trust increase.

Reaffirm the importance of individuality. Your daughter is a unique and wonderful person. She will think, feel, and look at the world differently than others. Assure her that difference of opinion or action is okay. If your daughter is a live wire and her friend is a shy bird, help her see the joy in both personalities. Explain that each personality has lots of layers, varied moments when the same person feels shy, energetic, sad, or thoughtful. What matters is the appropriateness of how we behave in a social situation. While she may be enthusiastic, your daughter needs to learn how and when to best express it. There is a difference between being yourself in appropriate situations and someone chiding you for wanting to be yourself at all. Help your daughter see the difference and celebrate her unique personality.

Direct her focus to discovering personal purpose. Children can change the world. For example, at the age of thirteen, Jayden Bledsoe started an IT company that by age fifteen he had turned into a $3.5 million global company. A seven-year-old boy found out African children had to walk miles for water and built a well in a Ugandan village (ultimately completing 667 projects). A thirteen-year-old boy wrote a New York Times Bestseller on how kids can do big things.

Your daughter has greatness within her. Each child does. Maybe she won't build a well or write a book, but becoming her bold, beautiful self and sharing it is just as magical. As you show her an expanded vision of herself and her life's possibilities, she will begin to develop a personal purpose. That in turn opens doors to developing her talents, meeting new people, and trying unique situations. Become aware of her strengths, even hidden ones. Encourage them without pressuring.

While talking with my daughter about all the possibilities there are for her in life, she shared that she's interested in training dolphins and orcas. I reassured her that it was something she could do. She became so excited that she immediately wanted to create a goal poster. Even if my daughter chooses a different career path, she has gained confidence that she can be herself and follow her dreams.

STARTER Qs

> ➤ Do you feel you can be yourself around others?
> ➤ What do you like best about yourself? What is one thing you want to change?
> ➤ When do you feel most afraid to be yourself? How do you handle that?
> ➤ What makes you feel that you matter? What do you want to do or feel that makes you feel more that way?

SCENARIOS

> ➤ You feel excited or hyper and start to be goofy. Your friends look at you funny or move away to do something else. What do you do?
> ➤ At recess, everyone wants to go walk around and gossip, but you want to play soccer. What do you say?

➤ One of your friends just created an amazing lemonade stand and made a ton of money. Yours didn't make hardly any. You feel like your projects or ventures never turn out. What do you do?

SUPER SENTENCES

My unique personality is great because

_____.

I can make a difference by

_____.

People say they love this about me:

_____.

When someone makes me feel badly for being me, I can say

_____.

One thing that helps me be my BEST ME is

_____.

Chapter 4: Mom and Me

Why do I fight more with my Mom? Does she not love me as much?
I want to be with my friends more than my mom. Is that bad?

As mentioned before, now that your daughter is officially twelve, more than just her body is shifting. Her emotions are conflicted because she is trying to reconcile the need for your support and love with the need to be independent and social. Beautifully, the more you lead the way in confidence and assurance, the more she will reflect the same. Now is the time for you to create intentional relationship patterns of respect, listening, and validation that will benefit you both for years to come.

Just for Mom Tips

Explain what's happening. Make your daughter aware that at this stage of life, she is naturally separating somewhat from you in order to feel more independent and individual. This is normal and even healthy, if done as kindly and effectively as possible. Help her understand that you are there for her, and that emotions make it hard to think clearly but that's what understanding and apologizing are for.

Reassure her your love is constant. Despite her mood swings and life confusion, you can be the anchor in that turbulent sea of hormones. Stay as unruffled as possible. Repeatedly share your love for her and about her. Remind your daughter what is good and unique and lovable about her. Some eye-rolling may be involved, but inside she will feed off of your confidence. In every conversation, try to find a way to insert one loving or appreciative statement to her (e.g., "You're such a big help to me," "I love being with you," "You brighten people's day, especially mine," or "I'm always so grateful I'm your mom.") This pays big dividends in the long run.

Take her feelings seriously. Says educator Lyn Mikel Brown, "One of the best things you can do for your daughter is not to assume she or other girls are, by nature, over-dramatic, mean, or gossipy... Appreciate and support your daughter's best impulses, praise her when she takes risks—especially if they involve going against the social tide—support her individuality, and downplay concerns about what other people think. Encourage her to be friends with a wide spectrum of people (without forcing the issue), and always, always assume the best—so will she."[8] As you validate her feelings, she will in turn be more willing to share them and listen to yours.

Get creative on ways to stay connected. Find the ideal way, time, and place that work to connect with your daughter. This may require some maneuvering. A friend of mine said when she was younger, she didn't talk much to her mother except right after school while her mother folded laundry. It wasn't until my friend was older that her mother confessed it was planned. She would get a laundry basket and position herself in the typical route of her daughter. When my friend walked in the door, her mother was casually and non-threateningly folding laundry. This allowed the daughter to open up. For you and your daughter, maybe it's late-night popcorn, mid-afternoon drives, sitting on the back porch, or pulling weeds together. Look for then, take the moment and stay connected!

STARTER Qs

> I've noticed we've seemed to be butting heads a little more lately. Have you noticed that at all? I'm not stressed about it, but I'm curious about why—any ideas?

> I'm so happy you've got good friends that you like being with. I've noticed we don't spend as much time together, and I want you to know that's okay. Can we find some ways to still get our talks in or spend a little time together?

> I've been thinking about how I can help you with this transition into sixth grade. I know you can do it by yourself, but I'd like to cheer you on and be there for you. Can you think of anything I can do or help with?

SCENARIOS

> You want to wear your sister's cute shirt that finally fits, but your mom says it's too low in the front. Again. It feels like she's always got to get in your business. How do you handle the different opinions?

➢ Your mom wants you to visit Grandma, but your friends have already asked you to come over for a party. What do you do?

➢ Sometimes just being with your mom feels awkward or stressful. When she asks you about it, you get defensive and angry and then yell. What can you do to express your feelings differently?

SUPER SENTENCES

I know my Mom loves me because

_____.

I can show my Mom I love her by

_____.

I like to spend time with friends doing

_____.

Instead of getting angry at my Mom, I can

_____.

I can use respectful words and phrases with my Mom like

_____.

Chapter 5: Puberty

When I have my period, will people still like me?

I feel emotional for no reason. Am I being a baby?

My body is doing some weird things. Is that normal?

Some girls are developing faster than I am. Is there something wrong with me?

While puberty is an incredible event for our children, it can also be a time of confusion, frustration, and misunderstandings. Your daughter will experience a variety of expected physical and emotional changes. As a mother, prepare your daughter by explaining the upcoming changes and how to best deal with them. Assure her the changes are normal, that all children go through them, and that there is nothing to worry about. Instead, she can celebrate it (maybe not shout for joy, but as much as possible). In reality, she is becoming a young woman and that means more responsibility and more joy. When you share about puberty from a perspective that is calm and makes her feel that "this is normal," she will take heart and more likely reciprocate.

Physical. Most children experience puberty between the ages of eight and fourteen and in four basic stages, according to British pediatrician, Dr. James Tanner. These changes include breast development (from buds to fully developed tissue), body odor development (generally around age thirteen and above), increased sweat and oil secretion, and emerging body hair (from baby-fine to adult-like).[9] She may also have vaginal discharge, which is harmless and simply a precursor to menstruation. Encourage your daughter to shower frequently and use deodorant as necessary.

When talking about these body shifts, use the right words and terminology. When my daughter and I spoke of maturation issues, I told her that while our personal body parts are sacred and special, explaining their purposes was not embarrassing. A vagina was not any more distressing than an elbow. If you do feel embarrassed, be open about it! She likely feels it, too. Say, "Wow, this is hard for me, give me a second. I'm really trying to get this right!" Your warmth and candor will put her at ease.

Emotional. The rapid growth in your daughter's brain, especially in the prefrontal and frontal lobes (the decision makers), affects her

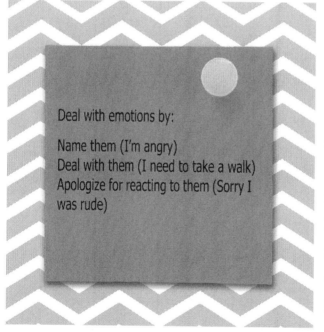

ability to manage her emotions. What may come across as resistant or rude is actually a physical rewiring process and a real-time normal testing of limits. When emotions intensify, what we call the "midbrain" takes over and rational thought leaves.[10] Survival is all that matters!

However, while mood swings come with the territory, healthy responses set the tone. Give your daughter, and yourself, a few useful tools.

Just for Mom Tips

Create awareness. Your role is to teach her how to be aware of her emotions and their shifts (what triggers the shift, how often, etc.). Ask her specific questions and show her the reality. For example, one of my daughters was having emotional meltdowns several times a day. Although I explained, encouraged, and endured, nothing changed. One day the idea came to have her write down when she had a mood swing. She wrote on a paper (none too willingly) the day and time, how she behaved, and what it was about. Within minutes another mood swing occurred, and we repeated the process. I still remember seeing that lightbulb go on in her mind—she finally got it, she was moody! This awareness lessened her mood swings and gave her a sense of control over herself.

Use your words. Help her describe what she is feeling and how to resolve it. You can use the template found in Chapter 5: "I feel _____ because_____ what I would prefer is_____"

Add humor. If you can lighten the mood appropriately, as well as show you're not reacting or escalating frustration, often your child will respond in kind. One day my daughter was behaving rather self-centeredly (*insert the word DIVA*). As I shared some thoughts on her being kind to the sibling she had offended, suddenly my daughter flung out her arms and rudely said, "What, so it's about *compassion* now?" We paused as that sentence hung in the air, and then we laughed ourselves silly. To this day it's a family funny.

STARTER Qs

➢ You're at an age when things are changing physically. Have you noticed anything different about your body?

➢ Body changes are normal, so if you're feeling anything different, that's totally fine. Mom's gone through those, too, weird as it sounds. You can ask me about anything—are there changes you want to know about? (If she says no, then share, "Super. I'd like to share just a couple so you have a heads up of what's coming." Ignore eye-rolling and expressions of "Ick.")

➢ I've noticed you've been just a tad emotional lately. Have you noticed it, too? Good news, it's totally normal. I thought it might be helpful to talk about why *and* why it's normal to tame the emotions, too.

SCENARIOS

➢ Your sister takes a set of your favorite earrings. Mentally, you know it's a small thing, but inside you feel this rage and urge to yell or smack her. What do you do?

➢ At school, a friend says that you said something you didn't. This has happened before. But today, it makes you burst into tears. You feel embarrassed to cry like that in front of other people. What do you say?

➤ Your mom and dad feel *so strict*. They won't let you have an opinion on anything or do anything without permission and all kinds of rules. You want to yell at them or slam your door and be alone. What can you do instead?

SUPER SENTENCES

I know my body is shifting and THAT IS GREAT!

I feel _____ because _____. I would prefer _____.

One way I can appreciate my body is

_____.

I can control my emotions by _____.

I can sincerely compliment others by saying positive things like

_____.

Chapter 6: Boys

Am I supposed to be dating or in a relationship with a boy at my age?

If a boy doesn't like me, does that mean I'm not pretty?

Why do boys try to act like they're all that and a bag of chips? Why are they annoying or aggressive?

There's no getting around it—by the age of twelve (and as early as seven and eight) your daughter is noticing boys. And they are likely noticing her. Such attention brings up all kinds of insecurities and self-image issues for girls. However, a healthy, connected relationship with Mom, combined with useful tools, can keep this part of life in proper perspective.

With this topic, vital to a healthy mother-daughter relationship is to keep open communication lines, but not to encourage inappropriate connection. It's a fine line. Also, it's important to help your daughter see herself as a whole person, not focused on the outside or fitting in.

Just for Mom Tips

Encourage friendships, not relationships. While some mothers say it's cute for their daughters to have crushes, studies show it's anything but cute. In the excellent book *Unsteady*, author JeaNette G. Smith shares how detrimental dating or a serious early love interest is to a girl's self-image and self-esteem. Don't encourage relationships or pairing off. Do encourage healthy hang-out time and connection with the opposite sex. Give her phrases or skills in responding to boys' overtures.

For example, during a Valentine's week at school, one of Connie's daughters, who is a fifth-grader, came home and said boys were asking her to be their Valentine. Her daughter's first reaction had been to say "NO!" to the boy, and in that serious of a tone. The problem? Young boys have fragile hearts. But she didn't want her daughter caught in early love triangles, however seemingly innocent. So she and her daughter devised a compromise—to a boy's Valentine request she would respond, "Yes, but only as friends." It worked for them.

Validate how she feels. Crushes can feel exactly like deeper love with many of the same symptoms, even though to parents it's simply "puppy love."[11] Affirm that she feels something new and different and that this is a normal part of growing up. Add that rejection is also part of the package and that affection or even kindness isn't always returned. Finish with the fact that at this stage, feelings are one thing, assertively acting on them another. That's what age and wisdom are for.

Set healthy limits. Talk clearly and openly with her about specifics (e.g. stay friends—which means no hand-holding, kissing, touching, etc.). If the crush is coming from the boy, give her words or phrases she can use such as, "I appreciate your feelings but I would like it if you stopped giving me notes. It makes me feel uncomfortable. I only want to be your friend." Nipping it in the bud gives your daughter clarity and confidence, now and in the future.

Teach her to be herself, not seek attention. If another girl is getting all the boy spotlight, tell your daughter not to worry. She is to keep focusing on developing herself and her talents, connecting with good friends, and enhancing her sense of humor. Share with her the long vision—at first she'll feel like an Ugly Duckling (read the story together or watch a modern movie spin-off). But in time not only will her realness create more confidence, but her solid self-identity will attract the attention of other healthy kids.

Be candid with boys about their behavior. In sixth grade, a boy respects a girl who can sling it right back—but without thoroughly bruising his ego (he is only twelve, after all). If a boy is bothering your daughter, it's possible he likes her. However, if his behavior has become very annoying, teach your daughter to retaliate without placing undue attention on him. These can be simple actions from your daughter such as giving him a look, getting up and moving to a new spot, or saying, "That doesn't feel good. Stop it." They speak a boy's direct language. He may or may not continue—if needed, involve the teacher.

STARTER Qs

> ➤ I know it's kind of personal, talking about boys, but I've noticed that you and your friends seem to talk about it sometimes. What boys are your friends? Are there any that are more than that? How do you feel about that at this age? Can I share with you how I feel?

> ➤ Sometimes boys are interested in someone as more than a friend, but that someone isn't interested back. Have you had

that experience at all? What did you do? If not and that happens to you, what do you think would be a good way to handle it?

➤ I was thinking about the new things you're dealing with this year and one of them is boys. Have you had any thoughts about that? Does it seem different to you this year than from last year? How do you handle friendships with the boys? What's working for you?

SCENARIOS

➤ A boy gives you a note that says he likes you. But you like him only as a friend. What do you do? (Hint: check out the phrases above.)

➤ You have a crush on a boy, but you know you're too young to do anything about it. You want to talk to your Mom, but you're afraid she won't understand and will be mad. What can you say?

➤ You overhear a few boys talking about a really pretty girl. Lots of boys talk about her. It makes you feel not very pretty. How do you handle the situation? What is the truth?

SUPER SENTENCES

I get healthy attention from others by

_____.

If a boy is annoying me I can

_____.

When I feel others are prettier, I remember

_____.

I like to focus on my talents of

_____.

I can stay friends with boys by

_____.

Chapter 7: Friends

How do I find true friends?

Should I try to make everyone else happy all the time?

How do I disagree with my friends? Will they hate me?

For mothers, sixth grade can be a bittersweet time. Perhaps you've shared a close relationship with your daughter so far, talking and connecting in simple and enjoyable ways. But once she enters this era, the pulling away begins. Suddenly, friends take precedence and have first rights on secrets and being the experts. It can be a tough transition for caring moms.

What's important now is to reassure her of your consistent and unchanging love. Though the physical and emotional realities mean adjusting, your love is constant. Giving your daughter that emotional bedrock will soothe and support her during the emotional rollercoasters sure to come.

Just for Mom Tips

Set healthy friendship limits. While friends are key at this age, family is still core. Validate her need to spend time with peers, but continue to require her participation in family time. Create a schedule that works for you, your child, and your family. Perhaps what's best is hanging out once during the school week and then twice on the weekends, or every other day, or for certain periods of time (three hours rather than six to eight hours). Healthy limits keep friend-time in the right balance. In the Sokol home, homework and daily chores need to be finished before friend-time begins. Encourage those healthy connections with a clear and consistent rule of how long and how often.

Teach her healthy friend behaviors. At this stage, drama rules, but it doesn't need to rule your life or your daughter's. Healthy behaviors that could be practiced at this age include listening, showing empathy, caring about someone's hurt feelings, speaking kindly, apologizing, and looking out for someone else. Teach her that girls are learning how to be in a group as well as be more independent. It's confusing to them, too. What helps is to share honest feelings, such as, "When you say I'm not your best friend anymore, it hurts my feelings. If you want to spend time with another friend, you can tell me that honestly."

Give her coping skills for tough situations. Help your daughter understand that all good and healthy relationships go through growing pains. Arguing with her best friend is not abnormal. But *how* she argues is key. Here are some good tips for positive communication:

Use "I" statements. When sharing feelings, she can use phrases like "I feel..." or "I'm not understanding x, y, or z," or "I felt hurt by..." Encourage her to use a kindly candid tone—not mean or belittling, but honest and calm.

Own your opinion. No two people are going to agree all the time—it's not realistic or healthy. Your daughter can use the "I" statements to state how she feels and then add, "What do you think?" After listening to her friend, she can follow up with something like "Hmm, I hadn't thought about that," or "That's interesting; I didn't know you thought that," or "Thanks for sharing." It doesn't mean she agrees, it means she's listening. If others pressure her to change her mind, she can use phrases like "I appreciate your opinion. Mine is different and that's okay," or "I don't want to do/say that," or "Since we can't agree, let's do/talk about something else right now."

Only you can make you happy. Girls tend to want to please, a wonderful trait that helps make the world a better and happier place. However, when girls feel they have to please in order to be liked, to be approved of, or to have friends, then behaviors become unhealthy. Help your daughter to understand the difference. Every person is responsible for their own happiness. If she has tried to be kind or do the right thing and someone else takes offense or is unhappy, that is their problem, not hers. She can use phrases like "I'm sorry you're sad. I don't feel I did or said anything wrong. I hope you feel better and we can still be friends," or "That hurt my feelings. I need a little break and some time to get back to feeling happy again."

STARTER Qs

> Which friend do you feel the most comfortable with and why?
> When you and your friends disagree, how do you girls handle it? How has that worked?
> What is your biggest worry right now about friends?
> If you had one thing you wanted to tell your friend right now, what would it be?

➢ I noticed you've wanted to spend more time with friends lately, and that's great. How often do you feel is good for you to hang out during the week?

SCENARIOS

➢ Addie is best friends with Jenna and asks her to hang out the next afternoon. Jenna says she can't; she's got homework. But Addie sees Jenna over at another friend's house during that same time. What should she do?

➢ Your friends are deciding which movie to go see. Everyone wants to see the newest release but you've been told it's got violence and scenes too scary for kids. You're embarrassed to say anything, and everyone wants to go, but inside you really don't want to. What do you say?

➢ Your friends Brittany and Lisa have been off-and-on friends for months. It hurts feelings when suddenly one or the other doesn't want to be together anymore. You want to be friends with both of them, but when they argue, they pull you into it by saying they won't be at your house if she is there. What is the best way to handle this?

SUPER SENTENCES:

I don't have to make others happy. By **being happy**, I make the world a happier place!

When friends disagree I can say

_____.

One way I can be a true friend is to

_____.

When others gossip, I can reply with

_____.

One way I can share my feelings with friends is to say, I feel

_____ about _____.

Chapter 8: Peer Pressure

Should I believe the mean things others say about me?

Who makes "popular groups" popular?

Should I try to be, look, and act like everyone at school to fit in?

In this day, children deal with more varied and intense peer pressure than ever before. They have greater access to and opportunities for trying harder drugs, alcohol, and premarital sex. And they face more vocal and widespread repercussions when they resist. One woman shared that when a third-grader had non-permitted Binaca breath spray at school, kids coerced people to try it with phrases like "Just try it," and "It's not going to hurt you." If someone refused, he or she was called names and was told that no one would be his or her friend. Studies show this negative peer pressure starts as young as nine.[12]

> Key phrases for you:
> "Help me understand..."
> "Can you share with me..."
> "Tell me how you see it..."
>
> Key phrases for her:
> "I don't have to do that to feel liked or popular."
> "I feel better when I do what I know is right."
> "It doesn't make sense to me that you're angry because I say no."
> "I feel good about not doing/saying that."

At the same developmental time, daughters are listening *more* to peers and separating from parents. Suddenly, you're a nerd. You know nothing. You're embarrassingly outdated. As James Lehman, MSW, shares, "The truth is, you can tell your child something every day and just get an argument. Then one day, his best friend tells him the exact same thing and now it's gospel."

Welcome to parenting a sixth-grader.

The good news is that studies show you still have great influence. One University of Sydney study found, "Parents and teachers who might feel powerless during adolescence have a bigger influence on academic motivation than they think—sometimes up to three times the impact of peers."[13] (Andrew Martin, an associate professor at the Faculty of Education and Social Work and the study's lead researcher.) The key seems to be positive parental connections. If kids had strong relationships, they seemed to respond better to peers. Consider these tips for connection and combatting negative peer influence.

Just for Mom Tips

Don't overreact. It's the old adage for parents of youth: if you like it, they'll loathe it. Whether it's a dirty word or a nose ring, stay neutral and share feelings from a thoughtful rather than angry place. Address the concern but in a calm and connecting way, e.g. "I care a lot about your friend, Sierra, and I'm concerned about some of the things she chooses to do and say. Help me understand what you feel when you're with her or what you hope for in this friendship." As you keep the communication lines open, she will typically work out the angst and questions in a healthy way.

Validate your child's need to be accepted. And not just accepted, but popular or well-liked. This isn't in her mind—studies show it's a serious part of the cultural norm and their survival as a sixth-grader.[14] Validate that need with phrases like "I know how important this is to you and kids your age..." or "I want you to feel accepted, too..." so she knows you're on her side. And follow up with healthy additions such as "I want you to recognize that more important and lasting is to be accepted by people who love and care about you."

Teach her how to deal with socially pressured situations. To instill self-confidence, teach her to use clear statements such as "I don't have to do that to feel good about myself," or "Everyone gets to make their own choices—I choose no on this one," or "Trying to make me feel bad because I say no isn't what a true friend would do."

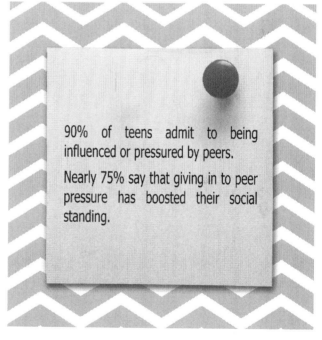

90% of teens admit to being influenced or pressured by peers.

Nearly 75% say that giving in to peer pressure has boosted their social standing.

Respond to bullying with clarity and consistency. If your daughter is being maligned, whether it's small-time gossiping or full-on cyberbullying, help her to address it decidedly. Ask her to talk with you or a trusted adult at the school (sometimes kids would rather tell someone else first). Let her know she has a voice and she can use it—that oftentimes will at least initially deter a bully. Especially with gossip, have her *directly address the person* who supposedly gossiped about her. The person is usually so embarrassed that she thinks twice before doing so next time, knowing she will likely be called out.

Lastly, take distinctive action to protect your child while giving her control. If she can use responsive phrases such as those shared above, a bully will see her sense of identity and often think twice before pursuing. Help your daughter know that people will always talk, even way past sixth grade. But as the adage goes, "What someone else thinks of you is none of your business." She is to hold her head high, smile, and respond with kind candor.

> In a recent study, researchers at the University of Southern California discovered that pressure to smoke is greater in middle school than in high school.
>
> Read more at: http://www.empoweringparents.com/Parenting-Teens-Parental-Authority-Vs-Peer-Pressure.php#ixzz3UtXvbDgT.

Show her that popularity is fleeting. Ask your daughter to name the most popular singer last year. Then two years ago. Then five years ago. Likely, she can't do it. Help her understand that it's a moment in time and then it's gone. Popularity is not real. Most often, popular opinion lasts as long as the person meets a need for someone else. When the need isn't met, the person is no longer popular. Years ago I remember reading a book with my young son. The main character was unique and interesting, but the popular kids pressured her to fit in, to act and dress like they did, and to talk about things they did. Against her better judgment she did every single thing they told her to do. What was the result? The popular kids *still* didn't accept her, because then she was too easily swayed, and she never was "one of them" to begin with.

Encourage your daughter to identify one to three friends that are true friends (read Chapter 6 for more insight). Qualities such as loyalty, kindness, trustworthiness, confidence, diligence, and being a hard-worker, amongst other qualities describe good friends. Then ask her to choose one friend and do one thing for her this week to show appreciation. As your daughter focuses on healthy connections, she will gain the strength needed to face down the popular peers who might otherwise railroad her good decisions.

STARTER Qs

> ➤ I noticed you've been spending more time alone lately. Is everything okay?

> ➤ I was reading this book the other day, and it mentioned peer pressure being worse now than when I was young. Do you think that's true? In what way?

➤ Have you dealt with people speaking rudely about you? How did you handle that? What did you do/say today?

➤ Kids sometimes talk about the "popular" group or being popular. What does that look like to you? Do you feel you have to change to be popular? What is one way you can be yourself and not try to prove yourself to that crowd?

SCENARIOS

➤ You just found out that a supposed "good friend" has been talking about you behind your back. What do you do?

➤ Every day the "popular" people sit together at lunch. You sit with a few trusted friends, but you still feel left out of the main group. What can you do about the situation? Why do you want to be with a popular group instead of the ones who already know and love you?

➤ One of the popular girls invites you to a party—but you can't bring your other friends and you have to dress in a way you don't like. Do you say something, and if so, what do you say?

SUPER SENTENCES

I know _____ is a good friend because she

_____.

I don't need to do wrong to feel right.

One way I feel secure is

_____.

I fight gossip and negative words by

_____.

One thing I can do this week to strengthen a true friendship is to

_____.

Chapter 9: School

I'm starting middle school/junior high and I'm scared. How do I handle the change?

I'm afraid sixth grade will be too hard. What if I fail?

Is it dumb to want to try out for things like honors classes, band, or sports?

Although we will address middle school in more detail in the "What Every 7ᵗʰ Grader Needs to Know" book, some children begin middle school in sixth grade. Talk about a huge adjustment: Kids go from one consistent teacher and one safe classroom to several teachers, many classes, a sea of people, and a ton of homework. Although the following will help your sixth-grader, read the seventh-grade book for particular help with these adjustments.

For those kids continuing in elementary school, your daughter is at the top of the heap. She's earned this place, and now, she wants to make the most of it. What your daughter needs most regarding school is a predictable experience at home, assurance she is smart and capable, and specific support as is helpful.

Just for Mom Tips

Prepare your child for success. Teach her now, before junior high, how to balance after-school activities and to prioritize her tasks (academics before play, chores before fun). She can learn to organize time and assignments by creating a tracking system (using notepads, iPads, sticky notes—whatever works best). Have her choose a rhythm—write to-dos in one place; do homework at a consistent time (e.g. 5:30 p.m. daily); reward her efforts as well as successes (a treat, points, play money to earn a prize, etc.). Do not overschedule her. In my *Back to Basics* book I share time-management tips that can help both mother and daughter wisely use their twenty-four hours.

Teach her to talk through it. As she gets older, your daughter will typically become better at verbalizing her feelings (whether she does with you or someone else). Discuss the sixth-grade school year, and even anticipating seventh-grade, from an emotional standpoint. She will feel some fear, anxiety, excitement, and worry about this new venture. Validate those feelings as normal, and encourage her to move forward with confidence that she can do difficult things. Brainstorm a few specific ways she can deal with the tasks or feelings that are a concern.

Affirm that being smart is okay. Too often kids, especially girls at this age, try to hide their intelligence or good grades. Girls especially learn as early as nine to minimize their academic abilities.[15] They feel pressured to focus on social relationships and being valued for appearance and social connection.

Validate your daughter's abilities with verbal compliments (e.g. "Terrific job using your noodle!" or "Excellent work developing your talents!"). Give fun rewards for extra-mile grades—for example, in the Sokol home As and Bs are considered the standard but straight As are an extra-mile achievement and are rewarded with a "Mom and Me" shopping day. Affirm that it's normal to do well at this age. If she receives flack, she can set the tone with her friends with phrases like "I like doing well" or "I want to become a _____ so I need to have good grades now."

Note: A sub-problem could be giftedness. One study found that over half of gifted children (IQs of 132 or above) were overlooked because of a focus on behavior problems. The brighter a child is the more likely she will feel out of place in a regular classroom, socially and academically. And the more she will try to hide it. An excellent book on giftedness is Bobbie Gilman's award-winning book, *Academic Advocacy for Gifted Children: A Parent's Complete Guide*[16].

Encourage the learning process. Let her know she has what it takes to be successful. This is because true success requires effort and consistency, both of which she can control. When she does well, add phrases like "Great job following directions" or "You were able to do it because you focused and stayed with it." When we simply say things like they're smart or clever, it teaches girls that either they innately have an ability (to do math, science, spelling words) or they don't. This can lead to feeling self-doubt and giving up.

SCENARIOS

> You're in a group of friends and someone shares their grades—the grades aren't very high. They laugh it off and mock a few of the "brainy" girls in class. Your grades are very good. What do you do?

> You're falling behind in math but you don't want to look dumb. Your friends don't seem to have a problem with math, and you're afraid to ask for help. How can you deal with this?

> Sometimes all that you need to do feels overwhelming. You've tried to stay organized, but it feels like people keep getting down on you for forgetting things or not doing as well as you have in the past. What can you say or do?

SUPER SENTENCES

I can do difficult things!

One tough experience or goal in my life that I did great in was

_____.

One way I can face a new situation with confidence is by

_____.

I can manage my time by

_____.

I can try new things, no matter the outcome. One thing I want to try is

_____.

Chapter 10: Dreams & Goals

I think I know what I want to be when I grow up, but can I change my mind later?

I want to do great things, but I'm not very good at setting goals. What if I can't achieve them?

What if people think my dreams and goals are dumb?

From Connie: In sixth grade, my teacher assigned us to make a booklet entitled All About Me. One paragraph was on what I wanted for my future life. I wrote down all my dreams, including that I wanted to be married in a blue dress and become a writer. Since then, I've achieved each one of those things I wrote (except that I married in a white dress, which proved to be a wiser choice).

As early as sixth grade (sometimes even before), it's vital that we mothers open our daughters to a vision of who they are and can become. Show her the big picture. Literally take a piece of paper and draw a Life Timeline. Draw a horizontal line with a vertical mark at one end labeled "birth" and a mark at the opposite end labeled "death." Then begin marking by increments of three, five, or ten years (five years in the early stages). Write new transitions such as: junior high, high school, drive, date, get a job, prepare for college, college, marriage, children, buy a home, etc. Showing her a snapshot of life's possibilities creates a perfect segue to the conversation of her dreams and goals.

An important start to the conversation is the difference between dreams and goals. A dream is something you deeply desire to do, become, or experience. A goal is a vehicle to make that happen. You need both to succeed! The dream provides the vision, the sometimes hazy view of the ultimate destination that can often be more of a feeling than a clear statement. The goal provides the daily how-to, the specific steps needed on the path to reach that destination.

Try this mini exercise with your daughter to develop her dreams and goals.

Create a Mini Life Plan. In my *Faithful, Fit & Fabulous* book, one chapter is devoted to simply and enjoyably creating a personal Life Vision. For your daughter, I've made this even easier.

1. Have her brainstorm words or phrases that describe her future ideal life (e.g. happy, money to do what she wants, travel to a certain place, be a mother, have a particular job like photographer or writer, etc.) This jumpstarts her creativity so no self-editing—write *all* her answers down!

2. Have her write, with a pencil on paper, a bubble diagram: in the middle she writes what is most important in her life (e.g. family). Then she draws a stick line out from the circle in another direction, draws another circle and writes the answer to another question (below). She continues to draw stick lines out and adding circles to help her see the life areas that matter to her.

What talents do you want to develop?

What kind of work do you want to do (e.g. photography, writing, hair-styling, medical, etc.)?

What do you want to do for fun?

How do you want to help others or make the world a better place?

What would you do if you had a whole year free from any to-dos?

What are some things you want to improve?

What are some physical goals (learn a sport, exercise in fun ways, eat healthier)?

What are dreams you want to achieve?

3. When finished, have her post it by her bed or in a special place for her to frequently see, consider, change, tweak, and develop. Let her know this is a simple way of actively pursuing her life.

Don't underestimate the power of this simple exercise. One night my daughter and I chatted about her future dreams. She mentioned wanting to train dolphins and orcas. As we approached it positively and realistically, her excitement increased to the point that she said, "Stop talking, Mom, I want to write my goal poster." And she did! Her dreams became more real to her, and she has a clearer idea of how to follow the path to achieve them. My daughter may or may not continue that path, but we have begun to instill the confidence and possibility she will need to follow her dreams in the future.

Just for Mom Tips

Encourage baby steps. No dream is achieved overnight, not even for adults. Teach her that success comes by degrees. Her job is to put time and effort into the chosen goals—from there she just needs to add in a little prayer and pixie dust! Also, the fruition of her goals may come in unexpected ways. Instead of taking a direct route, she may be led to several paths that ultimately get her where she wants to go. Lastly, the dream may change or morph into something she hadn't planned at all!

That is okay; in fact, it's wonderful! Dreams and goals are ways for us to discover, layer by layer, what we truly want from life and ourselves. They are not rigid, controlling must-dos that box us in.

Remind her of the realities. As mentioned, my daughter and I discussed the realities of working as a Sea World trainer with an orca. (*Mom's face masking immediate thoughts of deep peril*) They included the required schooling, emotional preparation, physical stamina, etc. I related achieving her dream to the here and now. For example, we talked of how learning to deal with a difficult sister was great preparation for dealing with difficult creatures (give or take). She made the connection and it shifted how she treated her siblings. As you get appropriately specific (don't overwhelm, give a realistic overview) she will begin to get the vision of what is required to succeed now and in the future.

Choose SIMPLE goals. Depending on your child's personality and interest, choose a few simple goals. Perhaps try three main goals for the entire year, or one goal a month, or at the most one goal a week. For example, with my daughter's goal to train animals, we broke it down into several smaller goals: find out what training requires; watch You Tube videos of training in action; visit Sea World to see the trainers live; contact trainers to see if she could visit backstage, etc. She also set life goals to support her personal development: get good grades (important for future hiring); get along with siblings (as said above); and to read scriptures and pray (to be open and inspired regarding opportunities). These clear, simple goals allowed her to focus on specific move-forward steps without being overwhelmed.

Keep dreams and goals forefront! Whether your daughter writes and posts them on a board, her wall, in a notebook, or on a sticky pad, make the goals visual. And keep talking about them! In the past, we have made family Life Mats. On placemat-size cardstock our children have written three dreams/goals for the year and then decorated the mat with their name, stickers, and drawings. I laminated the finished product and we used them for dinner placemats. That way we could easily and informally discuss their goals throughout the year in a family setting.

Encourage attempts. In my book *Motherhood Matters*, I share author J.K. Rowling's commencement speech for the 2008 Harvard graduating class. Her talk is on failure and its surprising power. She says, "Some failure in life is inevitable. It is impossible to live without failing at something, unless you live so cautiously that you might as well not have lived at all—in which case, you fail by default." That is your daughter at this stage. At the tail end of the cute-because-you're-trying stage, she can try many new interests to get a taste of her possibilities without having to fully commit for life. Give her opportunities. Cheerlead her efforts. Branch out in perspectives. Discuss some of her personal talents and decide how you can help. (For more on this subject, see Chapter 3.)

Dreaming and goal-setting are lifelong practices that bring joy and success at any age or stage. And particularly for moms and daughters! Continue to encourage this process and both of you will share in each other's growth journeys. At the time of writing this book, my mother invited me on a once-in-a-lifetime trip to return to Europe, where we originally lived. First, it was a dream that didn't seem initially feasible.

Then we moved forward as if it were possible. Lastly, we set and achieved small goals until the details were done. And now, it's a reality!

Start dreaming and goal-setting with your daughter today. Although your personal dreams and goals will be different, your supporting her at this age will yield lifelong fruits.

SCENARIOS

- ➤ Your daughter says she wants to be a crocodile catcher. You think this is very unwise. However, she is extremely passionate about it. What do you do?

- ➤ When talking with your daughter about goals, she gets easily overwhelmed. As you break it down into smaller "chewable" chunks, she still can't see how to do it. How do you encourage her?

- ➤ While discussing dreams and goals, your daughter shares an experience (or more) where she totally failed. It still bothers her, creating self-doubt, fear, and anxiety. What personal experiences can you share of overcoming fear, trying again, and ultimately succeeding?

- ➤ Your daughter says she shared her dream of being a crocodile catcher with her friends (or at school). People told her that her dream was dumb, that it wouldn't work, and that she was a loser. How do you respond?

SUPER SENTENCES

I can succeed because I know how to

_____.

My dream is to _____.

One goal that will help achieve my dream is

_____.

My mom can help me realize my dream by

_____.

I can do better at goal-achieving by

_____.

[Download a fun Weekly Goal sheet to post at www.coachmom.org or

www.conniesokol.com]

A Message from the Coach Mom Team of Connie & Rachelle:

We're delighted that you chose to pick up this book and read it. With so many choices, we're honored you chose ours.

Our goal at Coach Mom is to impact the world by empowering moms to make positive change. As a reader you can greatly increase that impact by simply reviewing this book on Amazon or Goodreads https://www.goodreads.com/book/show/25266537-what-every-6th-grader-needs-to-know, and other favorite places.

If you'd like early updates on new book releases or the rest of the series, please sign up for the Coach Mom newsletter at www.coachmom.org.

We love hearing from our readers. If you have questions or comments, please email us at contact@coachmom.org. While we cannot respond to every message, we do read them all. Thank you!

Lastly, we've provided a sneak peek of *10 Secrets Every 4th Grader Needs to Know: Tips & Tools to Connect Moms & Daughters*

Enjoy!

Rachelle J. Christensen & Connie E. Sokol

P.S. Here are extra resources:

For Rachelle:

Rachelle Facebook Author Page:
http://www.facebook.com/rachellechristensenauthor

Twitter: http://twitter.com/#!/rachellewrites

Instagram: #rachellewrites

Blog: http://rachellewrites.blogspot.com/

Author Website: http://rachellechristensen.com/

Goodreads Author Page:

https://www.goodreads.com/author/show/3327139.Rachelle_J_Christe nsen

Amazon Author Page for Rachelle:
http://www.amazon.com/Rachelle-J.-Christesen/e/B002UO5H48/ref=sr_ntt_srch_lnk_2?qid=1427567936&sr=1-2

For Connie:

Website: www.conniesokol.com (for more books, blogs, TV segments, and more)

Facebook: www.facebook.com/8basics

Twitter: @SokolConnie

Instagram: #sokolconnie

Amazon Author Page:
http://www.amazon.com/Connie-E.-Sokol/e/B00530YEVI/ref=sr_ntt_srch_lnk_1?qid=1427864271&sr=8-1

Goodreads Author Page:
https://www.goodreads.com/author/show/5032389.Connie_E_Sokol?from_search=true

Subscribe to the Coach Mom Newsletter: Website www.coachmom.org

Sneak peek of *What Every 4th Grader Needs to Know: 10 Secrets to Connect Moms & Kids*

I want to eat my lunch, but my friends are always rushing me to go play. What should I do?

Great job on recognizing your feelings! Yes, you should definitely eat lunch first because your body needs fuel to have fun. But you can still play too. Simply use the right words, like:

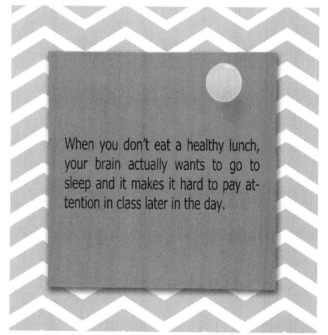

When you don't eat a healthy lunch, your brain actually wants to go to sleep and it makes it hard to pay attention in class later in the day.

- ❖ "I'm going to finish my lunch and then I'll be right out."
- ❖ "I'll play in a few minutes. Do you want to finish your lunch too? We can go out together after we eat."
- ❖ "I'm excited to play too. Why don't you go out, and I'll meet you by the basketball hoop as soon as I'm done?"

At first you might feel worried. It can feel like all the fourth-graders are leaving and you're the only one still eating lunch. That's okay! Enjoy every bite, chew slowly, and allow your body the chance to get energy. Then go out to recess and enjoy playing, running, and jumping.

My Thoughts...

About the Authors

Coach Mom is the fabulous coaching team of Rachelle Christensen, mother of five, and Connie Sokol, mother of seven. They have worked together to bring you the secrets to growing up happy, being excited about life, and loving yourself.

Rachelle J. Christensen is a mother of five who loves connecting with her children and wrote this book in answer to questions from her two daughters. She also has an amazing husband, three cats, and five chickens. An award-winning author, she has written several mystery/suspense novels, and she solves the mystery of the missing shoe on a daily basis. Rachelle graduated cum laude from Utah State University with a degree in psychology and a music minor. She enjoys singing and songwriting,  playing the piano, running, motivational speaking, and, of course, reading. Visit www.rachellechristensen.com to learn more about upcoming books.

Connie E. Sokol is a mother of seven and a favorite local and national speaker for over fifteen years. She is a core contributor on KSL TV's "Studio 5 with Brooke Walker" and a national blogger for "Motherhood Matters" at www.ksl.com. She is a former TV and radio host for Bonneville Communications and newspaper and magazine columnist. Mrs. Sokol is the author of twelve books including *Faithful, Fit & Fabulous*; *Create a Powerful Life Plan*; *The Life is Too Short Collection*; *40 Days with the Savior;* and *Caribbean Crossroads*. Mrs. Sokol marinates in time spent with her family and eating decadent treats. For her TV segments, blog, podcasts and more, visit www.conniesokol.com.

References

[1] Jill Churchill, "Quotable Quote," goodreads, https://www.goodreads.com/quotes/274570-there-s-no-way-to-be-a-perfect-mother-and-a..

[2] Gary and Joy Lundberg. *I Don't Have to Make Everything All Better*. Provo, UT: Penguin Publishing, 2000.

[3] "A Fifth of Girls as Young as 12 Won't Leave Home Without Full Make-up," DailyMail.com, http://www.dailymail.co.uk/femail/article-2723853/Would-YOU-let-12-year-old-wear-make-Over-HALF-14s-wear-EVERY-day-nearly-fifth-wont-leave-home-without-cosmetics-on.html#ixzz3UqfRMVSF.

[4] Geralyn B. Coopersmith, Fit and Female (Hoboken, NJ: Wiley, 2006), 14-15.

[5] Alyssa Detweiler, "9 Surprising Reasons Why You Should Smile More," inspiyr: live better, http://inspiyr.com/9-benefits-of-smiling/.

[6] Jill Suttie and Jason Marsh, "5 Ways Giving Is Good for You," GreaterGood: The Science of a Meaningful Life, http://greatergood.berkeley.edu/article/item/5_ways_giving_is_good_for_you.

[7] "Fast Facts," Teen Health and the Media—Body Image and Nutrition, https://depts.washington.edu/thmedia/view.cgi?section=bodyimage&page=fastfacts

[8] "Understanding Middle School Friendships," PBSparents, http://www.pbs.org/parents/parenting/raising-girls/friends-social-life/understanding-middle-school-friendships/.

[9] Tima M. St. John, M.D., "What Are the 4 Stages of Puberty?" Livestrong.com, http://www.livestrong.com/article/89098-stages-puberty/.

[10] "Your Sixth Grader," St. Anne School, http://www.stannesea.org/documents/Your6thGrader.pdf.

[11] Sandra Gordon, "How to Handle Your Child's First Crush," metro family: OKC Family Fun, http://www.metrofamilymagazine.com/September-2012/How-to-Handle-Your-Childs-First-Crush/.

[12] Malia Jacobson, "Peer Pressure: Why It Seems Worse Than Ever and How to Help Kids Resist It," ParentMap, https://www.parentmap.com/article/peer-pressure-why-it-seems-worse-than-ever-and-how-to-help-kids-resist-it.

[13] "Parents and Teachers Have More Influence Than Peers," The University of Sydney, http://sydney.edu.au/news/84.html?newsstoryid=3392.

[14] "Parents and Teachers Have More Influence Than Peers," The University of Sydney, http://sydney.edu.au/news/84.html?newsstoryid=3392.

[15] Heidi Grant Halvorson, Ph.D., "The Trouble with Bright Girls," Psychology Today, https://www.psychologytoday.com/blog/the-science-success/201101/the-trouble-bright-girls.

[16] Linda Silverman, "What We Have Learned about Gifted Children," gifted development center: embracing giftedness, http://www.gifteddevelopment.com/articles/what-we-have-learned-about-gifted-children.

Made in the USA
Lexington, KY
11 October 2018